silky little knits

ALISON CROWTHER-SMITH

silky little knits

Luxurious Designs and Accessories in Mohair-Silk Yarns

Trafalgar Square Books
North Pomfret, Vermont

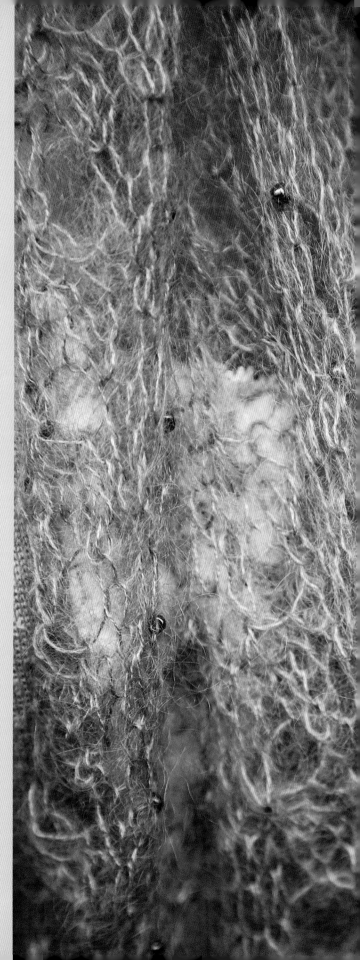

This book is dedicated to Mark William Crowther-Smith,
who has sweetly tolerated my yarn habit for so many
years and who says that upon my headstone he will place:
"Let me just finish this row..."

Silky Little Knits

First published the United States of America in 2009
by Trafalgar Square Books
North Pomfret, Vermont 05053

Editor Sally Harding
Designer Anne Wilson
Stylist Susan Berry
Pattern checker Emma King
Photography John Heseltine

Associate Publisher Susan Berry

ISBN 978-1-57076-441-7

LIbrary of Congress Number: 2009902039

Reproduced in Singapore
Printed in Singapore

contents

introduction

If I could take only one yarn to a desert island, it would be a fine luxury mohair-silk yarn like Rowan *Kidsilk Haze*—or it's slightly thicker cousin Rowan *Kidsilk Aura*. I also love designing and knitting accessories. That could be my short attention span kicking in again, or it might be a simple fact of life: we love to knit but very often time limits us to accessories. And they do make perfect gifts!

So having established that mohair and accessories would be a great combination, the next step for me when planning this book was to demonstrate how artful this yarn can be. My collection of mohair-silk accessories is about the many—often very simple—ways that mohair can be used to maximize its impact.

Knitting with fine mohair-silk yarn is often described by knitters as like knitting with cobwebs. It's beauty is evident, even in a plain stockinette stitch piece. The sheen of the silk structure and the haze of the mohair combine to make the simplest design glow. Lace stitches in fine mohair-silk yarn become even more ethereal, although I think that simple lace patterns work the best since the beauty of the yarn does half the work for you. You can see the eyecatching effect of mohair lace in my Gathering Scarf on page 68 as well as the Lucia Beaded Wrap on page 100.

Rowan's fine *Kidsilk Haze* and their medium-weight *Kidsilk Aura* are my favorite mohair-silk yarns not only because of their high quality, but also because of their extensive color palette. And one of the great versatilities of mohair yarns is that you can easily extend an original color range by blending shades together in a most creative and exciting way. With a lightweight yarn, holding two or even three strands together still yields quite a fine knitted fabric. I have experimented with various color-mixing methods in this collection, from a basic blending of two similar shades, such as on the Frilled Bedsocks (see page 42), to more complex colorwash designs, such as on the Colorwash Pillow cover (see page 16) and the Stella Shrug (see page 72).

Another advantage of mohair is that you can add it to other yarns that have a different texture. In this collection, I have used Rowan *Kidsilk Haze* together with a wool tweed yarn in a pair of mittens to give a firmer yet very glamorous fabric (see page 91). I have also knitted *Kidsilk Haze* flowers and leaves to decorate a simple trellis scarf knitted in a cotton-mix yarn (see page 65). The Latticework Lace Scarf on page 78 uses a combination of *Kidsilk Haze* and a pure cotton yarn; here the mohair-silk really softens the cotton and the cotton gives a firmer definition to the mohair—it's still a very delicate piece, but warmer and with more substance.

Finally, mohair yarn is perfect for other decorative effects. Introducing beads and sequins to mohair-silk designs adds a very feminine and delicate sparkle (see the bag on page 35). Because of the sheer nature of the yarn, beads appear to "float" on the surface of mohair lace (see page 68). Frills and frilly flowers are gorgeous in this yarn, too (see pages 58 and 111). In fact, it's almost impossible to say the word "frill" without immediately thinking of fine mohair-silk yarn!

My aim is to introduce you to lovely mohair-silk yarn through these accessories and to help you gain the confidence to experiment with your own ideas.

Alison Crowther-Smith

gallery of luxury-mohair samples

This gallery of samples is just a small selection of the many different effects you can achieve with luxury mohair-mix yarns such as Rowan *Kidsilk Haze* and Rowan *Kidsilk Aura* and similar yarns. For these swatches, I have used different stitch patterns and color combinations, and mixed in other yarns and embellishments. They are all worked on size 6 (4mm) needles, except for the lace ones. Why not try them yourself and use them as a starting point for your own luxury-mohair design ideas?

LACE EFFECTS

Knitted lace always looks great in mohair. The arrowhead lace swatches below show how different the same lace stitch can look just with a change of needle size. You can also create a lace effect with mohair by knitting stockinette stitch on really big needles—it's as simple as that!

COLOR EFFECTS

Because you can create new colors by using two shades of mohair together, you can have a lot of fun with color effects. One of my color effects swatches on the opposite page uses two toning shades of mohair, which produces a beautiful subtle amalgam of the two original shades. Both shades look more intense and together they

really create a totally new color! This is the way you can blend colors to produce colorwash effects—gradually changing from one close color to another. But you can also mix together colors that contrast either in color or lightness-darkness for a marled or tweedy effect as in my other color effects swatch.

TEXTURAL EFFECTS

Mohair is ideal for mixing with other yarns to create contrasting textural effects. The swatches here show alternating stripes of mohair and a cotton-wool yarn. The cozy fluff of the mohair stands out beautifully against the soft, smooth wool-cotton mix. The simple stripes would make a perfect pillow cover and the chevron pattern a lovely lap throw.

DECORATIVE EFFECTS

To me, mohair just cries out for frills and beads. I often use both in my designs. You knit the tight frill by increasing quickly over only a few rows, working twice into all stitches on each right-side row. The beaded swatch uses subtly toning matt beads. Wouldn't it be lovely for a lined evening bag or a stole?

Lacy effects 1 (above): Arrowhead lace pattern worked in Rowan *Kidsilk Haze*; knitted with size 3 (3.25mm) needles.

Lacy effects 2 (above): Arrowhead lace pattern worked in Rowan *Kidsilk Haze*; knitted with size 8 (5mm) needles.

Color effects 1 (right):
One strand of Rowan *Kidsilk Haze* Trance and one strand of Storm used together.

Color effects 2 (far right):
One strand each of Rowan *Kidsilk Haze* Storm and Rowan *4-Ply Cotton* used together.

Textural effects 1 (right):
Simple alternating stripes of Rowan *Kidsilk Aura* and Rowan *Wool Cotton*.

Textural effects 2 (far right): Chevron stitch pattern in alternating stripes of Rowan *Kidsilk Aura* and Rowan *Wool Cotton*.

Decorative effects 1 (right):
Beaded Rowan *Kidsilk Aura*.

Decorative effects 2 (far right): A frill worked in Rowan *Kidsilk Aura*.

9

tips for knitting with luxury mohair

Mohair-mix yarns, especially those made of super-fine kid mohair and silk like Rowan *Kidsilk Haze* and *Kidsilk Aura*, are unique and beautiful hand-knitting yarns. The lightweight mohair-mix yarns like Rowan *Kidsilk Haze* have many applications, the best being those that utilize the fine, downy, quality. Thicker mohair-mix yarns like Rowan *Kidsilk Aura* are just as versatile. On both of these Rowan yarns the silk forms the core of the yarn, with the kid mohair spun around the silk thread.

I am going to focus on the finer mohair-mix yarns for this section on successful knitting with these yarns, because they are the yarns that knitters can feel a little anxious about, and the tricks that work for lightweight mohairs apply to the medium-weight versions as well.

The main advantage of fine mohair is its versatility. For example, the needle sizes on the yarn label for Rowan *Kidsilk Haze* are sizes 3–8 (3.25–5mm). In fact, I also use larger needle sizes on fine mohair with great results, up to size 10½ (6.5mm) for some designs. Worked on small needle sizes, it yields a tight yet airy fabric; used double, it makes a very warm and more substantial fabric, while still retaining the loft for which mohair is renowned.

Fine mohair can also be used with other yarns to good effect. Try knitting it held together with a cotton-mix yarn such as Rowan *Calmer*; with a medium-weight wool-mohair yarn such as *Kid Classic*; or with a super-bulky yarn such as *Big Wool*. The resulting textures are excellent and adding the thin mohair doesn't alter the original gauge of the thicker yarn much. To get a dramatic tweed, use two contrasting colors of fine mohair. To get a subtle marled effect, use two toning colors.

Fine mohair is also excellent for knitting a detail on other yarns, such as an added frill, edging, collar, or flower feature.

People are sometimes concerned that lightweight mohair-mix yarn is difficult to knit with. It isn't difficult, just different. Because it is so fine, it takes a few rows to feel comfortable with it, and it needs careful handling, because of the hairy mohair fluff. These long fibers can catch on each other, but knowing this you will soon get the hang of it. It feels as if you are knitting with cobwebs, which takes a bit of getting used to.

These are my top tips for successful mohair knitting:

Dealing with long mohair fibers: Beware of the long mohair fibers which will occasionally masquerade as the actual yarn strand. Sometimes, a long and thick fiber lying across the needle, can look like a stitch and I have been caught out by this several times. With practice, you will quickly identify such rogue "stitches." Knit in really good light that casts little shadow, and try using needles that contrast with the yarn—dark metal or wood for light-colored yarn, light metal or wood for darker yarn.

Casting on: Use the right cast-on. The lace cast-on is best for many mohair-silk designs (see page 114), but the pattern will usually specify. A conventional thumb or cable cast-on gives a nice firm lower edge (see pages 76 and 95). However, if the design is lace and the lace is the lower edge of the item, such as a scarf, then the lace method for casting on is best. When you are going to pick up and knit into the cast-on edge of the item, for example, to knit an added frill or border, or if you will need to seam along this edge, then the thumb method will be best but you need to keep it fairly loose.

Your knitting tension: While you need to match the gauge of the pattern if it's for a garment, for accessories like scarves it is not the end of the world to be a bit out. And I recommend that you try and keep your yarn-holding tension slightly loose with mohair-mix yarn. Relax and do not pull your knitting too tight; if you feel it's tightening up or you are anxious, stop knitting, step away from the yarn and come back later!

Binding off: You will usually want the cast-on and the bound-off edges to match, so bind off loosely; if you just can't, then bind off with a bigger needle size.

Practice makes perfect: Practice with the yarn before you start the pattern, sacrificing a bit of the yarn to get the feel of it before you start the item itself. On a garment, this will be the gauge swatch.

Knitting lace patterns: If you are attempting a lace pattern and the pattern is also a bit of new challenge, knit a section of the pattern repeat for a few rows with a plain, fine cotton yarn on size 3 (3.25mm) needles—a yarn such as Rowan *4-Ply Cotton* is ideal. Then you will have mastered any tricky stitches before you start with the mohair.

Adding beads and sequins: Beads and sequins are "made" for mohair-silk yarn, but they can easily move about on the fine yarn and make their way to the back of the work. So purl over any beads *firmly* on the return row to keep them at the front. Both large and small beads look great on mohair, but if they are for an all-over beaded design, I often go for small beads as large beads can drag down this fine yarn. Sequins are tricky to work with and do not always want to lie flat—but they do look adorable on Rowan *Kidsilk Haze* and are worth using.

Threading on beads: When beading, don't overload the yarn with all the beads. Put on one or two hundred, but when they run out, break the yarn, thread on more beads and rejoin the yarn. This saves stressing the yarn by having hundreds of beads moved over it as you work. (See page 23 for more about bead knitting.)

Unraveling mohair knitting: The truth is, you really can't unravel mohair easily. If you go wrong, your best chance is to carefully TINK it back (KNIT backward) to the place where the error is. Taking it off the needles and pulling out the loops is not going to work, as the mohair fibers will catch and you'll get a ball of really angry mohair. I'd TINK back for several rows rather than pull it out. Alternatively, and especially if it's lace, see if you can run down the rows with a crochet hook to correct an error or recover a dropped stitch.

Felting mohair-mix yarns: Mohair-content yarn will felt readily and cannot be felted on its own. If you knit it held together with a different yarn, so you are knitting two strands, and then felt the item, it will increase the liability of the fabric to felt. So if you want felt, test it first and if you don't want felt, you will have to hand-wash that item each time.

Adding mohair details to garments: A very plain garment such as a fitted or semi-fitted cardigan in cotton or wool, can be transformed by picking up and knitting a simple narrow mohair-silk border all around the bottom, front opening, back neck, and sleeve edges. Pick up stitches with the right side facing, then on the next row bind off knitwise. Then knit a simple mohair-silk corsage in the same shade as the edge and pin on.

Mixing colors: Knitting with two strands of a fine mohair-silk like Rowan *Kidsilk Haze* gives a great effect, especially if you use two very different shades as on the mittens on page 82 or the bedsocks on page 42. Experiment with the effects contrasting or toning shades can give you, because you can create a whole new color palette by mixing yarns.

colorwash mittens

One of my favorite techniques for Rowan *Kidsilk Haze* is to use it to make up my own colors and blend them smoothly together. These mittens use three strands of different colors held together, and I created the striking colorwash effect by dropping and adding in the three shades gradually. Because of the greens, blues, and brown that I chose, the design looks really organic.

Knitted flat and joined with a side seam that leaves a gap for the thumb, the mittens are especially easy to knit, even for a beginner. If you want to start with an even easier pair, also knitted flat but using only one strand of yarn, try the mittens on pages 108 and 109.

SKILL LEVEL
Easy

SIZE OF MITTENS
Women's size medium; to fit palm circumference 17in/18cm. The finished mittens measure approximately 8³/4in/22cm from cast-on edge to frill.

WHAT YOU NEED
Rowan *Kidsilk Haze* in five colors as follows:

A 1 x ⁷/8oz/25g ball in browny green (588 Drab)
B 1 x ⁷/8oz/25g ball in lime green (597 Jelly)
C 1 x ⁷/8oz/25g ball in light sage (581 Meadow)
D 1 x ⁷/8oz/25g ball in pale blue-green (640 Glacier)
E 1 x ⁷/8oz/25g ball in dark blue-green (582 Trance)
Pair of size 6 (4mm) knitting needles

GAUGE
22 sts and 28 rows to 4in/10cm square measured over St st using three strands of yarn held together and size 6 (4mm) needles *or needle size necessary to obtain correct gauge.*

ABBREVIATIONS
See page 116.

SPECIAL PATTERN NOTE
The mittens are worked with three strands of yarn held together throughout. The colors are mixed together, so sometimes three strands of the same color are used together, sometimes two strands of one color and one strand of a different color are used, and sometimes one strand each of three different colors are used together. The colors used are abbreviated as follows:
If the patterns calls for AAA, use 3 strands of A held together; if it calls for AAB, use 2 strands of A and 1 strand of B held together; if it calls for ABB, use 1 strand of A and 2 strands of B held together; and so on.

TO MAKE MITTENS (make 2)
Using size 6 (4mm) needles and AAA (see Special Pattern Note above), cast on 39 sts with thumb or cable cast-on method (see pages 76 and 95).
Beg single rib as follows:
Rib row 1 K1, *P1, K1; rep from * to end.
Rib row 2 P1, *K1, P1; rep from * to end.
Rep last 2 rows once more.
Cont in rib as set (and cutting off and joining in strands as required), work in rib in stripes as follows:
Work 4 rows in AAB.
Work 4 rows in ABB.
Work 4 rows in BBB.
Work 4 rows in BBC.
Work 4 rows in BCC.
Work 4 rows in CCC.
Beg with a K row, work in St st in stripes as follows:
Work 4 rows in CCD.
Work 4 rows in CDD.
Work 4 rows in DDD.
Work 4 rows in DDE.
Work 4 rows in DEE.
Work 4 rows in EEE.
Work 4 rows in EEA.
Work 2 rows in EAA.
Still using EAA, work 2 rows in single rib.
Using AAA, work 4 rows more in single rib.
Using AAA, bind off in rib.
Make second mitten in exactly same way.

FRILL
With RS facing and using size 6 (4mm) needles and BCE, pick up and knit 32 sts evenly along bound-off edge of one mitten (see page 88).
Work frill as follows:
Row 1 (WS) P to end.
Row 2 K into front and back of each st to end. *64 sts.*
Row 3 P to end.

Row 4 K into front and back of each st to end. *128 sts*.
Bind off loosely knitwise (with WS facing).
Work frill on second mitten in same way.

TO FINISH MITTENS
Weave in any yarn ends.
Press the mittens very lightly on the wrong side, avoiding
the frill and referring to the yarn label for the pressing
instructions. (See page 116.)

Fold each mitten in half with right sides facing and the
side edges aligned; then sew the side seam, leaving a gap
of the right length, and in the right place, for your thumb.
Turn the mittens right side out and slip on!

colorwash pillow

The colorwash on this pillow is achieved in the same way as the coloring on the mittens on pages 12–15, by mixing three strands of yarns of different shades together throughout. I loved the look of the mittens so much that I thought that with a broader stripe, the colorwash effect would make a cozy pillow with real impact, and it does.

Take time to select a backing fabric for the pillow that looks great with your knitting. I backed my pillow with some Amy Butler Rowan fabric (*Primrose* in Aqua from the Nigella range), which tones with, yet also offers a vibrant contrast to, the soft and misty knitted front.

SKILL LEVEL
Easy

SIZE OF PILLOW
The finished pillow cover measures approximately 19in/47.5cm square.

WHAT YOU NEED
Rowan *Kidsilk Haze* in five colors as follows:

A 2 x ⁷/₈oz/25g balls in browny green (588 Drab)
B 2 x ⁷/₈oz/25g balls in lime green (597 Jelly)
C 2 x ⁷/₈oz/25g balls in light sage (581 Meadow)
D 2 x ⁷/₈oz/25g balls in pale blue-green (640 Glacier)
E 2 x ⁷/₈oz/25g balls in dark blue-green (582 Trance)
Pair of size 8 (5mm) knitting needles
Piece of cotton fabric 20in/50.5cm square, for pillow cover back, and matching sewing thread
Pillow form to fit finished cover

GAUGE
16 sts and 24 rows to 4in/10cm square measured over St st using three strands of yarn held together and size 8 (5mm) needles *or needle size necessary to obtain correct gauge.*

Alison's tip

• I like the contrast of the fabric back and the knitted front on pillows, but you could knit the back instead, making it either plain—using three strands of one color—or the same as the front.

ABBREVIATIONS
See page 116.

SPECIAL PATTERN NOTE
The pillow cover is worked with three strands of yarn held together throughout. The colors are mixed together, so sometimes three strands of the same color are used together, sometimes two strands of one color and one strand of a different color are used, and sometimes one strand each of three different colors are used together. The colors used are abbreviated as follows:
If the patterns calls for AAA, use 3 strands of A held together; if it calls for AAB, use 2 strands of A and 1 strand of B held together; if it calls for ABB, use 1 strand of A and 2 strands of B held together; and so on.

PILLOW COVER FRONT
Using size 8 (5mm) needles and AAA (see Special Pattern Note above), cast on 76 sts with thumb or cable cast-on method (see pages 76 and 95).
Beg with a K row (and cutting off and joining in strands as required), work in St st in stripes as follows:
Work 6 rows in AAA.
Work 6 rows in AAB.
Work 6 rows in ABB.
Work 6 rows in BBB.
Work 6 rows in BBC.
Work 6 rows in BCC.
Work 6 rows in CCC.
Work 6 rows in CCD.
Work 6 rows in CDD.
Work 6 rows in DDD.
Work 6 rows in DDE.
Work 6 rows in DEE.
Work 6 rows in EEE.
Work 6 rows in EEA.
Work 6 rows in EAA.
(This 90-row stripe sequence is repeated to form St st stripe patt.)

Cont in stripe patt as set until front measures 19in/
47.5cm from cast-on edge, ending with RS facing for
bind-off.
Bind off knitwise.

TO FINISH PILLOW COVER

Weave in any yarn ends.
Press the knitted front very lightly on the wrong side,
referring to the yarn label for the pressing instructions.
(See page 116.)

Pillow cover back

Cut a piece of fabric to the same size as the finished
knitted front, plus an extra ¹/₂in/1.5cm all around the
edge for the seam allowance.
With the right sides facing, sew the fabric back to the
knitted front along three sides, taking a ¹/₂in/1.5cm seam
allowance on the fabric and stitching close to the edge
on the knitting. Turn the cover right side out, insert the
pillow form, and sew the last side closed.

gleam evening wrap

Weighted down with a generous sprinkling of carefully placed beads, this is an ideal evening wrap for a cool night. The beading goes quite close to the edges of the shawl and their weight helps to overcome the curling that always affects stockinette stitch scarves. I used large crystal beads but you could easily get a slightly lighter, yet still beautiful, effect by using smaller beads—and, of course, there are so many beads and shades of Rowan *Kidsilk Haze* yarn to choose from.

The wrap is finished with a deep and gentle frill at each end, upon which you work very random beading to make a scattered effect. This is very easy knitting and the beading just becomes second nature as you get into the rhythm of the piece.

SKILL LEVEL
Easy

SIZE OF WRAP
The finished wrap measures approximately 22in/
55cm wide by 49½in/123.5cm long, when laying flat
unstretched and excluding frills.

WHAT YOU NEED
3 x ⁷/₈oz/25g balls of Rowan *Kidsilk Haze* in lime green
(597 Jelly)
Pair of size 9 (5.5mm) knitting needles
Approximately 1,700 crystal 4mm glass beads (Rowan
ref: large clear bead J3001008)

GAUGE
16 sts and 22 rows to 4in/10cm square measured over
beaded St st using size 9 (5.5mm) needles *or needle size
necessary to obtain correct gauge.*

ABBREVIATIONS
bead 1 = bring yarn to RS of work between the
2 needles, slide the bead up next to st just worked, slip
next stitch purlwise from LH needle to RH needle, then
take yarn back to WS of work between the 2 needles,
leaving bead sitting on RS of work in front of slipped st.
See also page 116.

TO MAKE WRAP
Thread approximately 540 beads onto each ball of yarn
before beginning the ball (see opposite page).
Using size 9 (5.5mm) needles, cast on 88 sts loosely, with
thumb cast-on method (see page 76).
Row 1 (RS) K1, *bead 1, K7; rep from * last 7 sts,
bead 1, K6.
Row 2 P to end.
Row 3 K5, *bead 1, K7; rep from * last 3 sts, bead 1, K2.
Row 4 P to end.
(Last 4 rows are repeated to form bead patt.)

Rep rows 1–4 until wrap measures approximately 49½in/
123.5cm from cast-on edge, ending with RS facing for
bind-off. (You will need about half of a ball for the frills, so
make sure you don't use too much for the wrap.)
Bind off loosely knitwise, trying to match looseness of
bound-off edge to that of cast-on edge.

TO FINISH WRAP
Weave in any yarn ends. Then before adding frill, press as
for the Gleam Shawl on page 26.
Frill
Thread half of the remaining beads onto the yarn.
With RS facing and using size 9 (5.5mm) needles, pick up
and knit 80 sts evenly along cast-on edge of wrap (see
page 88).
Row 1 (WS) P to end.
Row 2 (RS) *K3, K into front and back of next st; rep from
* to end. *100 sts.*
Row 3 and all WS rows P to end.
Row 4 *K9, bead 1; rep from * to last 10 sts, K10.
Row 6 *K4, K into front and back of next st; rep from * to
end. *120 sts.*
Row 8 *K9, bead 1; rep from * to last 10 sts, K10.
Row 10 *K4, K into front and back of next st; rep from *
to end. *144 sts.*
Row 12 *K9, bead 1: rep from * to last 14 sts, K10,
bead 1, K3.
Row 14 *K3, K into front and back of next st; rep from *
to end. *180 sts.*
Row 16 *K9, bead 1; rep from * to last 10 sts, K10.
Row 17 P to end.
Picot edging
Work the picot bind-off on the RS as follows:
*Using lace cast-on (see page 114), cast on 3 sts onto LH
needle, bind off 6 sts knitwise, transfer st on RH needle
back onto LH needle; rep from * to end and fasten off.
Thread the remaining beads onto the yarn and work frill
along bound-off edge in same way.
Weave in any yarn ends. Do not press frills.

knitting with beads and sequins

This is an invaluable technique and one that I am sure you will use to adorn all your luxury-mohair knitting. Beads and sequins are positioned in the same way, although sequins do not lie down as obediently and neatly as the beads, unless you get sequins with holes at one side rather than in the middle. If you want clusters of beads, thread on more to start with and move and position two or three beads together.

If you are using a bead on top of a sequin, you carry it out exactly the same as for the single bead or sequin, just move them along together. However, if you want the bead on top of the sequin, which you will, you must thread them on in the right order. Remember that whatever you thread on LAST will be the FIRST item to come off the yarn. So you must start threading with a bead and end with a sequin: bead, sequin, bead, sequin, and so on.

1 Thread on the beads or sequins before you cast on with the yarn. To do this, thread a fine sewing needle with a short length of sewing thread. (Check first that the beads and sequins you have chosen will fit over this needle.) Tie the two ends of the thread together to form a loop and hang the tail-end of your yarn through the loop. With the tip of this needle, pick up the bead or sequin and pass this along the needle, down the thread, and thus onto the yarn; you can pick up several beads or sequins together. (If you need to use hundreds of beads on a single ball of yarn, you can add them gradually, breaking the yarn each time you need to add more.)

2 When you want to place a bead or sequin, which will appear in the pattern at "*bead 1*" or "*place sequin and bead*," bring the yarn to the front (the right side) of the work between the two needles. Then slide a bead or sequin (or a sequin and bead together) up close to the stitch just worked. Slip the next stitch purlwise from the left-hand needle to the right-hand needle, inserting the right-hand needle from right to left through the front of the stitch. Then take the yarn back to the wrong side of the work as shown here, leaving the bead or sequin sitting on the right side of the work on top of the slipped stitch. The pattern will now state what you need to do next, usually knit the next stitch.

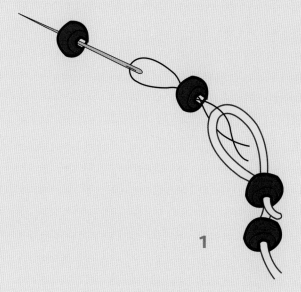

1

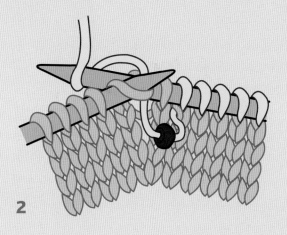

2

gleam shawl

A super-sized version of the beaded wrap on page 20, this is knitted in the thicker Rowan *Kidsilk Aura* for extra warmth and impact. What it loses in ethereal waft, it gains in snuggle and, as the yarn is a member of the *Kidsilk* family, the shawl still retains its glamour and beauty.

To me this shawl says "autumn walks" and it is very cozy, indeed. If anything, the knitting is even easier than on the *Kidsilk Haze* version because *Aura* is a thicker yarn and not as hairy. Also, I have reduced the number of beads and given the frill more of a finishing flare. You could easily whip through this project in a weekend and be wearing it by Monday evening.

SKILL LEVEL
Easy

SIZE OF SHAWL
The finished shawl measures approximately 20½in/51cm wide by 50½in/126cm long, when laying flat unstretched and excluding frills.

WHAT YOU NEED
9 x ⁷/₈oz/25g balls of Rowan *Kidsilk Aura* in raspberry red (760 Quarry Tile)
Pair of size 10 (6mm) knitting needles
Approximately 800 crystal 4mm glass beads (Rowan ref: large clear J3001008)

GAUGE
17 sts and 19 rows to 4in/10cm square measured over St st using size 10 (6mm) needles *or needle size necessary to obtain correct gauge.*

ABBREVIATIONS
bead 1 = bring yarn to RS of work between the 2 needles, slide the bead up next to st just worked, slip next stitch purlwise from LH needle to RH needle, then take yarn back to WS of work between the 2 needles, leaving bead sitting on RS of work in front of slipped st. *See also page 116.*

SPECIAL PATTERN NOTE
For tips on how to thread beads easily onto yarn, turn to page 23.

TO MAKE SHAWL
Thread approximately 88 beads onto each ball of yarn before beginning the ball.
Using size 10 (6mm) needles, cast on 87 sts loosely, with thumb cast-on method (see page 76).
Row 1 (RS) K3, *bead 1, K7; rep from * last 4 sts, bead 1, K3.

Row 2 P to end.
Row 3 K to end.
Row 4 P to end.
Row 5 *K7, bead 1; rep from * to last 7 sts, K7.
Rows 6, 7 and 8 Rep rows 2, 3 and 4.
(Last 8 rows are repeated to form bead patt.)
Rep row 1–8 until wrap measures approximately 50½in/126cm from cast-on edge, ending with RS facing for bind-off. (You will need about one and a half balls for the frills, so make sure you don't use too much for the shawl.)
Bind off loosely knitwise, trying to match looseness of bound-off edge to that of cast-on edge.

TO FINISH SHAWL
Weave in any yarn ends.
Block and press this piece of knitting, by pinning work, with the wrong side facing upward, onto a towel on the ironing board or table. Lay a damp cloth over the knitting and using a medium temperature iron, very gently skim over the damp cloth, using almost no pressure, holding

Alison's tip

• Make sure you only put as many beads as you need on each ball—about 85 plus a few extra to take account of varying gauge. Alternatively, thread on only half this number of beads before starting each ball and break the yarn when you need to put on the other half—you'll have more ends to sew in, but with fewer beads to push along the yarn, you might find the knitting easier.

the iron so it barely touches the cloth—do not press down at all! Remove the cloth. Leave the knitting pinned out until it is totally dry.

Frill

Thread half of the remaining beads onto the yarn.

With RS facing and using size 10 (6mm) needles, pick up and knit 86 sts evenly along cast-on edge of shawl (see page 88).

Row 1 (WS) P to end.

Row 2 (RS) *K2, K into front and back of next st; rep from * to last 2 sts, K2. *114 sts.*

Row 3 P to end.

Row 4 *K2, K into front and back of next st; rep from * to last 3 sts, K1, K into front and back of next st, K1. *152 sts.*

Row 5 P to end.

Row 6 K2, *bead 1, K5; rep from * to end.

Row 7 P to end.

Row 8 *K5, bead 1; rep from * to last 2 sts, K2.

Bind off loosely purlwise.

Thread the remaining beads onto the yarn and work frill along bound-off edge in same way.

Weave in any yarn ends.

Do not press frills.

starry beaded cape and corsage

This is a short elbow-length cape with a frilled lower edge and collar. It is gently shaped throughout, giving it a soft bell-like drape. Picked up and knitted edge-to-edge borders and a slightly flared collar, to which I naturally added a few beads, finish this stylish knit.

I knitted the cape and its matching corsage in a classic icy duck-egg blue, but there are so many shades of Rowan *Kidsilk Haze* to choose from and it's really such a straightforward knit that you may find you need several to go with your various dresses. Knit the matching evening bag on page 34 to complete the look. The corsage works up quickly, and it makes a nice gift.

Cape: Intermediate
Corsage: Easy

SIZE OF CAPE

Finished cape measures approximately 16¼in/41cm
long from the neck to the bound-off edge of the bottom
frill (approximately elbow length).

WHAT YOU NEED

3 x ⅞oz/25g balls of Rowan *Kidsilk Haze* in pale blue-
green (640 Glacier)
Pair of size 8 (5mm) knitting needles
Pair of size 6 (4mm) knitting needles
Size 8 (5mm) circular knitting needle, 32in/80cm long
Approximately 295 crystal 4mm glass beads (Rowan ref:
large clear bead J3001008)
Large safety pin or brooch-back, for corsage

GAUGE

18 sts and 22 rows to 4in/10cm square measured over
St st using size 8 (5mm) needles *or needle size necessary
to obtain correct gauge.*

ABBREVIATIONS

bead 1 = bring yarn to RS of work between the
2 needles, slide the bead up next to st just worked, slip
next stitch purlwise from LH needle to RH needle, then
take yarn back to WS of work between the 2 needles,
leaving bead sitting on RS of work in front of slipped st.
See also page 116.

SPECIAL PATTERN NOTE

For tips on how to thread beads easily onto yarn, turn to
page 23.

cape

TO MAKE CAPE

Using size 8 (5mm) needles, cast on 297 sts loosely, with
thumb or cable cast-on method (see pages 76 and 95).
Beg with a K row, work in St st until cape measures
6in/15cm from cast-on edge, ending with RS facing for
next row.
Next row (RS) K16, *K2, K2tog, K5, K2tog, K17; rep from
* to last st, K1. *277 sts.*
Cont in St st until cape measures 9in/23cm from cast-on
edge, ending with RS facing for next row.
Next row (RS) K16, *K1, K2tog, K5, K2tog, K16; rep from
* to last st, K1. *257 sts.*
Cont in St st until cape measures 12¼in/31cm from
cast-on edge, ending with RS facing for next row.
Next row (RS) K16, *K2tog, K5, K2tog, K15; rep from *
to last st, K1. *237 sts.*
Work 3 rows in St st, so ending with RS facing for
next row.
Next row (RS) *K3tog; rep from * to end. *79 sts.*
Change to size 6 (4mm) needles and work 5 rows more
in St st, so ending with RS facing for bind-off.
Bind off loosely knitwise.

RIGHT FRONT BEADED EDGING

Thread 22 beads onto yarn before picking up stitches
with it.
With RS facing and using size 8 (5mm) needles,
pick up and knit 67 sts evenly up right front edge of
front opening (see page 88).
Work 3 rows in garter st (knit every row), so ending with
RS facing for next row.
Next row (RS) K1, *bead 1, K2; rep from * to end.
Bind off very loosely knitwise.

LEFT FRONT BEADED EDGING

Thread 22 beads onto yarn before picking up stitches
with it.

With RS facing and using size 8 (5mm) needles, pick up and knit 67 sts evenly down left front edge of front opening.

Work 3 rows in garter st (knit every row), so ending with RS facing for next row.

Next row (RS) *K2, bead 1; rep from * to last st, K1.
Bind off very loosely knitwise.

NECK FRILL

With RS facing and using size 8 (5mm) needles, pick up and knit 114 sts evenly along neck edge (including along beaded edgings).

Next row (RS) K to end.

Alison's tips

• The beaded edgings on each side of the front of the cape must be bound off very loosely. If you find it difficult to bind off so loosely and at the same time evenly, use a bigger needle size—a size 10 (6mm)—to bind off with.

• When there are lots of stitches and lots of rows to work before you come to a beading row, as on the cape frills, it is a good idea not to thread the beads on before beginning the frill. Instead, to avoid having them on the yarn all the time, cut off your yarn right before starting the beading row, then thread on the beads, and rejoin the yarn. This way, you have more ends to sew in but it's easier knitting and causes less wear on the yarn.

Next row P to end.
Next row *K1, knit into front and back of next st: rep from * to end. *171 sts.*
Work 3 rows in St st, so ending with RS facing for next row.
Next row (RS) *K1, knit into front and back of next st; rep from * to last st, k1. *257 sts.*
Next row P to end.
Cut off yarn and thread 64 beads onto remaining yarn, then rejoin yarn and cont as follows:
Next row K1, *bead 1, K3; rep from * to end.
Bind off loosely purlwise.

LOWER-EDGE FRILL

With RS facing and size 8 (5mm) circular needle, pick up and knit 350 sts evenly along lower edge of cape.
Working back and forth in rows on circular needle, work frill as follows:
Row 1 (WS) P to end.
Row 2 (RS) *K1, K into front and back of next st; rep from * to end. *525 sts.*
Work 3 rows in St st, so ending with with RS facing for next row.
Next row (RS) *K2, K into front and back of next st; rep from * to end. *700 sts.*
Work 5 rows in St st, so ending with RS facing for next row.
Cut off yarn and thread 175 beads onto remaining yarn, then rejoin yarn and cont as follows:
Next row (RS) K1, *bead 1, K3; rep from * to last 3 sts, bead 1, K2.
Bind off loosely purlwise.

TO FINISH CAPE

Weave in any yarn ends.
Press cape very lightly on the wrong side, avoiding the frills and referring to the yarn label for the pressing instructions. (See page 116.)

corsage

BASE FLOWER

Using size 6 (4mm) needles and 2 strands of yarn held tog, cast on 60 sts with lace cast-on method (see page 114).

Row 1 (RS) K to end.

Row 2 P to end.

Rows 3, 4, 5, and 6 [Rep rows 1 and 2] twice.

Row 7 (RS) K6, *rotate RH needle once clockwise (turning it right over so the work between the needles is twisted), K6; rep from * to end.

Row 8 P to end.

Row 9 *K2tog; rep from * to end. *30 sts.*

Row 10 *P2tog; rep from * to end. *15 sts.*

Row 11 K1, *K2tog; rep from * to end. *8 sts.*

Cut off yarn, leaving a long yarn tail, thread this yarn tail onto a blunt-ended sewing needle, and thread tail back through 8 sts on knitting needle, slipping sts off knitting needle as you proceed. Pull yarn end to gather sts and secure.

TOP FLOWER

Using size 6 (4mm) needles and 2 strands of yarn held tog, cast on 42 sts with lace cast-on method (see page 114).

Row 1 (RS) K to end.

Row 2 P to end.

Rows 3 and 4 Rep rows 1 and 2.

Row 5 (RS) K6, *rotate RH needle once clockwise (turning it right over so the work between the needles is twisted), K6; rep from * to end.

Row 6 P to end.

Row 7 *K2tog; rep from * to end. *21 sts.*

Row 8 P1, *P2tog; rep from * to end. *11 sts.*

Row 9 K1, *K2tog; rep from * to end. *6 sts.*

Cut off yarn, leaving a long yarn tail, thread this yarn tail onto a blunt-ended sewing needle, and thread tail back through 6 sts on knitting needle, slipping sts off knitting needle as you proceed. Pull yarn end to gather sts and secure.

TO FINISH CORSAGE

Weave in any yarn ends.

Sew the flowers one on top of the other, with the "star" points offset. Sew three clusters of four beads each into center of flower.

Sew a large safety pin or brooch-back to the wrong side of the corsage.

Alison's tips

• The petal-like edges on the base and top flowers of the corsage are created with a very interesting technique. You work the first rows of the flowers in stockinette stitch in the usual way. Then to achieve the wavy edge, you twist the knitting between the needles after every sixth stitch to make a petal shape. On the next few rows of the flower the stitches are decreased to gather the knitting together.

• I have made the corsage for the cape in the same shade of yarn, but if you want it to stand out more, you could knit it in a contrasting color or knit each layer in a different shade. The corsage is so easy to knit that it would be fun to make several and use them on other knits.

aurora evening bag

I have knitted this confection of an accessory in pale blue-green to match the evening cape and corsage on page 28, but you can make it in whatever shade you prefer. It's really dainty, so not much room for more than a cellphone and a lipstick.

When knitting frivolous goodies with Rowan *Kidsilk Haze*, what is even more gorgeous than beads? Yes, beads and sequins—together! I grant you that it takes patience, but the effort is well rewarded because of the sparkly result. Less sparkle needed? Just place a bead or a sequin on it's own where I have placed a bead and sequin together. Still less sparkle? Just knit a stitch where I have placed the jewels.

My beads and sequins are icy silver to tone well with the cool yarn color. However, hot pink yarn, pink sequins, and black beads look lovely together, and rather saucy, too. If, like me, you have been blessed with the glitter-gene, experiment with this great technique.

SKILL LEVEL
Intermediate

SIZE OF BAG
The finished bag measures approximately 7in/18cm wide by 6 1/2in/16cm tall from bottom edge to beginning of frill.

WHAT YOU NEED
2 x 7/8oz/25g balls of Rowan *Kidsilk Haze* in pale blue-green (640 Glacier)

Pair of size 6 (4mm) knitting needles

A spare size 6 (4mm) knitting needle to bind off with

1 stitch holder

Approximately 204 crystal 3mm glass beads (Rowan ref: large clear bead J3001008)

204 silver sequins, 10mm in diameter (Gutterman ref: sequin 773824)

Piece of fine lining material to match yarn, approximately 8 1/2in/22cm by 18in/46cm, and matching sewing thread 27 1/2in/70cm of 5/8in/1.5cm wide ribbon, for drawstring-strap

GAUGE
22 sts and 29 rows to 4in/10cm square measured over beaded St st using two strands of yarn held together and size 6 (4mm) needles *or needle size necessary to obtain correct gauge.*

ABBREVIATIONS
PS&B (place sequin and bead) = bring yarn to RS of work between the 2 needles, slide a sequin-and-bead together up next to st just worked (so that the bead sits on top of the sequin), slip next stitch purlwise from LH needle to RH needle, then take yarn back to WS of work between the 2 needles, leaving bead-sequin sitting on RS of work in front of slipped st.
See also page 116.

SPECIAL PATTERN NOTES
The technique for threading and knitting the bead-plus-sequin together is the same as for beads on their own, which is explained on page 23. Note, however, that whatever you thread onto your yarn LAST, comes off the yarn FIRST—of course. So you must start threading with a bead and end with a sequin: bead, sequin, bead, sequin, and so on.

The bag is worked with two strands of yarn held together throughout, so thread beads and sequins onto both strands before casting on.

FRONT OF BAG
Thread 2 strands of yarn (held together) with half (102) the beads and sequins in this order: *bead, sequin; rep from * to end of beads and sequins, ending with a sequin.

Using size 6 (4mm) needles and 2 strands of yarn held tog (the yarn with beads and sequins threaded on it), cast on sts with the *picot cast-on* as follows:

*Using lace cast-on method (see page 114), cast on 6 sts onto LH needle, bind off 3 sts, transfer st now left on RH needle to LH needle; rep from * until there are 78 sts on LH needle. *78 sts.*

Row 1 (RS) K to end.

Row 2 P to end.

Row 3 *K2, PB&S; rep from * to last 3 sts, K3.

Row 4 P to end.

Row 5 *K2tog; rep from * to end. *39 sts.*

Row 6 P to end.

This completes the frill.

Row 7 (RS) P to end (to form foldline).

(**Note:** From now on even-numbered rows become RS rows as the RS and WS are reversed after the frill.)

Row 8 (eyelet row) (RS) *K3, yo, K2tog; rep from * to last 4 sts, K4.

Row 9 P to end.

Row 10 K to end.

Rows 11–14 [Rep rows 9 and 10] twice.

Row 15 P to end.

Row 16 *K3, PB&S; rep from * to last 3 sts, K3.

Row 17 and 18 Rep rows 9 and 10.

Row 19 P to end.

Row 20 K5, *PB&S, K3; rep from * to last 6 sts, PB&S, K5.

[Rep rows 13–20] 3 times, then [rep rows 13–19] once, so ending with RS facing for next row.

Beg with a K row, work 2 rows in St st.

Cut off yarn and place sts on a st holder.

BACK OF BAG

Work exactly as for Front of Bag, but leave sts on needle and do not cut off yarn.

TO FINISH BAG

Transfer stitches of Front of Bag onto a size 6 (4mm) needle.

Postion the Front and Back with right sides facing, with the Front nearest you and the needles aligned.

Using a spare size 6 (4mm) needle, bind off sts of Front and Back together as follows:

Insert spare needle through first st of Front and first st of Back and, using yarn still attached to Back, K these 2 sts tog, *K next st on each needle tog in same way, bind off 1 st; rep from * to end.

Weave in any yarn ends.

Using a slightly damp cloth and a cool iron, press the knitting very lightly on the wrong side—be careful not to press the iron down or rest it on the work of the sequins will melt! Do not press the picot edge and frill. (See page 116.)

Lining

Cut a piece of fabric to the same size as the joined knitted Front and Back up to the frill foldlines, plus an extra ¹/₂in/1.5cm all around the edge for the seam allowance. Fold the lining fabric in half widthwise and sew the side seams.

With right sides together, sew the side seams of knitted bag together, up to the eyelet holes. Turn the bag right side out.

Insert the lining inside the knitted bag. Then turn under the seam allowance at the top of the lining and hand sew the folded edge at top of the lining to the inside of the knitted bag, ensuring that the fabric will come up over the top of the eyelet row. You will have to ease in the knitting here as it will feel very stretchy.

From the right side and using a safety pin, thread the ribbon through the eyelets and pull to close the bag. The ribbon also forms the strap.

Alison's tips

• The cast-on and bound-off stitches that you make in the picot cast-on, form the sides of the little picot "fingers" so you want them to match in tension, otherwise they will bend.

• Be sure to read the Special Pattern Note on the opposite page before beginning your knitting, so you thread on the beads and sequins in the right order.

• When knitting-in the bead-sequin combo, position the bead firmly as close as possible to the hole in the middle of the sequin, but don't pull too tightly. You can always nudge the beads into the middle of the sequins later.

• The fabric lining in the bag is essential, but it is easy sewing and and can be done all by hand—or by machine, except for the hand stitches that join it to the top of the bag.

linda beaded boa

Lime green and black has been a big fashion story for several seasons now and this certainly has color impact. The boa is knitted in two layers, so you can elect to knit it in your own favorite shades, or knit the two layers in the same color. It is really a rather delicate boa, unlike it's big sister on page 50.

Yes, I know the number of stitches you end up with to make the frills twist and flare may seem daunting, but console yourself with the thought that because it is knitted sideways—there are very few rows! Beads are only introduced at the end of each layer, although you know I will be the last person to discourage you from adding more if you wish.

My beloved picot bind-off makes a further appearance, and though it takes ages, it's essential to complete this delicate piece.

SKILL LEVEL
Easy

SIZE OF BOA
The finished boa measures approximately 58¼in/148cm long.

WHAT YOU NEED
Rowan *Kidsilk Haze* in two colors as follows:
A 3 x ⅞oz/25g balls in lime green (597 Jelly)
B 2 x ⅞oz/25g ball in black (599 Wicked)
Size 8 (5mm) circular knitting needle, 32in/80cm or 39in/100cm long
Approximately 350 crystal 4mm glass beads (Rowan ref large clear bead J3001008)

GAUGE
There is no need to work this boa to a specific gauge. The final length will vary slightly from knitter to knitter, which won't matter at all.

Alison's tip

• When casting on so many stitches at once—like you have to for this boa—the recounting after the cast-on can be difficult. The best thing to do to make it easier is to cast on the first 100 stitches and recount them, place a stitch marker on the needle, then cast on another 75 stitches and recount them. Slip the marker off when you come to it in the first row.

ABBREVIATIONS
bead 1 = bring yarn to RS of work between the 2 needles, slide the bead up next to st just worked, slip next stitch purlwise from LH needle to RH needle, then take yarn back to WS of work between the 2 needles, leaving bead sitting on RS of work in front of slipped st. *See also page 116.*

SPECIAL PATTERN NOTE
For tips on how to thread beads easily onto yarn, turn to page 23.

FIRST FRILL LAYER
Using size 8 (5mm) circular needle and A, cast on 175 sts.
Working back and forth in rows on circular needle throughout, beg as follows:
Row 1 (RS) K into front and back of each st to end of row. *350 sts.*
Row 2 P to end.
Row 3 K to end.
Row 4 P to end.
Row 5 K into front and back of each st to end of row. *700 sts.*
Row 6 P to end.
Row 7 K to end.
Row 8 P to end.
Row 9 K to end.
Row 10 P to end.
Row 11 *K1, K into front and back of next st; rep from * to end. *1,050 sts.*
Row 12 P to end.
Cut off yarn and thread half the beads onto remaining yarn A, then rejoin A and cont as follows:
Row 13 K2, bead 1, *K5, bead 1; rep from * to last 3 sts, K3.
Picot edging
Work the picot bind-off on WS as follows:
*Using lace cast-on method (see page 114), cast on 3 sts

onto LH needle, bind off 6 sts knitwise, transfer st on RH needle back onto LH needle; rep from * to end and fasten off.

SECOND FRILL LAYER

Hold First Frill Layer with RS facing and cast-on edge uppermost, then using size 8 (5mm) circular needle and B, pick up and knit 175 sts evenly along cast-on edge (see page 88).

Row 1 (RS) K into front and back of each st to end of row. *350 sts.*

Row 2 P to end.

Row 3 K to end.

Row 4 P to end.

Row 5 K into front and back of each st to end of row. *700 sts.*

Row 6 P to end.

Row 7 *K1, K into front and back of next st; rep from * to end. *1,050 sts.*

Row 8 P to end.

Cut off yarn and thread remaining beads onto remaining yarn B, then rejoin B and cont as follows:

Row 9 K2, bead 1, *K5, bead 1; rep from * to last 3 sts, K3.

Picot edging

Work the picot bind-off on WS as follows: *Using lace cast-on method, cast on 3 sts onto LH needle, bind off 6 sts knitwise, transfer st on RH needle back onto LH needle; rep from * to end and fasten off.

TO FINISH BOA

Weave in any yarn ends. There is no need to press.

frilled bedsocks
and gift bag

Cozy and gorgeous: glamour can also be practical! These warm yet light socks are knitted in two closely linked shades of pink, one soft and one vibrant. The two colors are used together for the main part of the socks and then the colors are used separately for the frills at the top.

If you have never knitted socks in the round before, then apart from the yarn being held double, this is such an easy pattern. If the words "turn the heel" have put you right off, forget your worries. This is easy—just follow the pattern step by step, and soon you, too, will be in the sock-knitting fraternity. But yours will be these gorgeous bedsocks, not big rugged going-out-for-a-hike socks.

Knit the gift bag if you intend to give your socks away as a gift.

SKILL LEVEL
Intermediate

SIZE OF SOCKS AND GIFT BAG
Socks: The socks are a good snug fit for a women's size 7½ (UK size 5) and measure 8¼in/21cm from back of heel to end of toe unstretched, but you can adjust the length by adding to or subtracting from the number of rounds (see Alison's Tips on opposite page).
Gift bag: The finished bag measures approximately 4½in/11cm wide by 6½in/16.5cm tall, exluding frill.

WHAT YOU NEED
Rowan *Kidsilk Haze* in two colors as follows:
A 2 x ⅞oz/25g balls in light rose pink (583 Blushes)
B 2 x ⅞oz/25g balls in hot pink (606 Candy Girl)
Set of four size 1 (2.5mm) double-pointed knitting needles
3 stitch markers, all in different colors—yellow, green, and red (or tie on different colors of yarn for your stitch markers)
30in/75cm of ⅜–⅝in/1–1.5cm wide ribbon
2 large safety pins for "cheat's" toe bind-off

GAUGE
36 sts and 40 rows to 4in/10cm square measured over St st using one strand each of yarns A and yarn B held together and size 1 (2.5mm) needles *or needle size necessary to obtain correct gauge.*

ABBREVIATIONS
See page 116.

SPECIAL PATTERN NOTES
The socks and gift bag are made using one strand each of yarn A and yarn B held together throughout—this is called AB in the pattern.
The frills, however, are made using a single strand of yarn.

socks

TO MAKE SOCKS (make 2)
Using size 1 (2.5mm) double-pointed needles and AB (see Special Pattern Note above), cast on 60 sts and distribute these sts over 3 needles—placing 20 sts on each needle (see page 48).
Making sure cast-on sts are not twisted, hold 3 needles in a ring ready to beg first round and place a yellow stitch marker on right needle at end of cast-on sts to mark beg/end of round.
Using 4th needle to knit with, beg ribbing at top of sock as follows:
Round 1 (RS) *K1, P1; rep from * to end of round.
(Last round is repeated to form single rib.)
Cont in rib as set (slipping marker when reached throughout) until a total of 21 rib rounds have been completed.
Work in St st (knit every round) for 23 rounds.
Heel flap
You will now begin working in conventional St st (knit RS rows and purl WS rows) as you will be working flat on 2 needles just for the heel flap.
Next row (RS) K15, turn.
Next row (WS) Sl 1, P29, turn.
Do not remove yellow marker, but keep slipping it throughout.
Place the rest of the sts on spare needles.
Cont on these 30 sts only for the heel flap as follows:
Next row Sl 1, K29, turn.
Next row Sl 1, P29, turn.
Rep last 2 rows 13 times more, so ending with a WS row.
Next row (RS) Sl 1, K29, turn.
Turn heel
No panicking now! All we are doing is a little gentle decreasing and shaping so the sock goes nicely around your heel. Cont as follows:
Next row Sl 1, P16, P2tog, P1, turn.
Next row Sl 1, K5, skp, K1, turn.

Next row Sl 1, P6, P2tog, P1, turn.

Next row Sl 1, K7, skp, K1, turn.

Next row Sl 1, P8, P2tog, P1, turn.

Next row Sl 1, K9, skp, K1, turn.

Next row Sl 1, P10, P2tog, P1, turn.

Next row Sl 1, K11, skp, K1, turn.

Next row Sl 1, P12, P2tog, P1, turn.

Next row Sl 1, K13, skp, K1, turn.

Next row Sl 1, P14, P2tog, P1, turn.

Next row Sl 1, K15, skp, K1, do NOT turn.

You now have 18 sts on the needle.

Create foot top

With RS still facing at end of last row and using set of double-pointed needles, pick up and knit 15 sts down the side of the heel flap and place a marker (you will need to be able to identify this marker as Marker No. 1—I use a green one here, green for "go"); K the 30 sts left over from the cuff that you have had waiting all this time and place a marker (you will need to be able to identify this marker as Marker No. 2—I use a red one here, red for "stop"); pick up and K another 15 sts from other side of heel flap; K to yellow marker (beg/end of round); and now distribute all these sts over 3 needles. *78 sts.*

Shape foot

You are now going back to working in the round and knitting every round to cont in St st as follows:

Next round K to within 3 sts of Marker No. 1, K2tog, K1, slip marker; K to Marker No. 2, slip marker, K1, skp, K to end of round.

Next round K to end.

Rep last 2 rounds until there are 60 sts again and redistribute sts equally on 3 needles if necessary (the number of sts between Marker Nos. 1 and 2 will not vary, the decreasing is taking place on the other side of the markers).

Work foot

Keeping markers in place, work 45 rows more in St st (knit every round) or to suit length of foot (see Alison's Tips, right).

Alison's tips

• You can adjust the socks to fit your foot size. Just knit the sock up to where it says "Work foot." Then work the section that goes from the start of your instep to where the toe shaping begins; this pattern calls for 45 rounds here, but you can adjust this to the length you require—40–48 rounds will probably fit most women's shoe sizes. But remember that the socks will stretch at least $1/2$–$3/4$in/ 1.5–2cm to accommodate your foot.

• As well as adjusting the length of the socks to fit your foot, you can also adjust the circumference of the sock once you become familiar with how to turn the heel. On these socks when you create the top of the sock you have a total of 78 stitches—18 from the recently turned heel, plus 15 from one side of heel flap, 30 from the original cuff, and 15 from the other side of the heel flap. So you can see how easy it would be to increase or reduce the numbers to get bigger or smaller socks. After you have made a couple of pairs for yourself, you may want to try making them for other members of your family!

• The length of the sock ribbing and the length of the sock from the bottom of the heel to the cast-on edge is also adjustable. Just work more rib rows and/or more stockinette stitch rows before beginning the heel flap.

Shape toe

Next round K to within 3 sts to Marker No. 1, K2tog, K1, slip marker, K1, skp; K to within 3 sts of Marker No. 2, K2tog, K1, slip marker, K1, skp, K to end of round. *56 sts.*

Next round K to end.

Next round K to within 3 sts to Marker No. 1, K2tog, K1, slip marker, K1, skp; K to within 3 sts of Marker No. 2, K2tog, K1, slip marker, K1, skp, K to end of round.

Rep last 2 rounds until there are 28 sts (if you want a more "pointy" toe, cont until there are 24 sts).

Next round K to first marker and stop.

Distribute 28 sts equally on 2 needles (14 sts on each needle), remove all markers, and make sure the working yarn is at one end, ready to go, by knitting there if needs be.

You can graft or Kitchener stitch the toe seam now, or you can cheat delightfully as follows:

Cut off yarn, leaving a nice long tail to bind off with (about 12in/30cm).

Slip the sts onto 2 large safety pins, then turn sock inside out and slip sts back onto 2 needles.

Hold the 2 needles with the sts on them together, and using 3rd needle, knit the first st on each needle together as one; knit the second sts tog in same way, and slip the first st on the RH needle over the 2nd st and off the RH needle to bind off the first st in the usual way.

Cont casting off in this way until all sts are bound off.

Make second sock in exactly same way.

OUTER FRILLS

With RS facing and using size 1 (2.5mm) double-pointed needles and 1 strand of A, pick up and knit 60 sts around outside of cast-on cuff-top edge on one sock (see page 88), working into the outer loops of the cast-on sts when picking up sts and distributing sts over 3 needles.

Place a stitch marker on needle at beg of round (slipping it when reached throughout), then using 4th needle to knit with, beg frill as follows:

Round 1 (RS) K to end.

Round 2 K into front and back of each st. *120 sts.*

Rep last 2 rounds once more. *240 sts.*

Bind off loosely knitwise.

Work outer frill on other sock in exactly same way.

INNER FRILLS

Turn one sock inside out and with WS facing and using size 1 (2.5mm) double-pointed needles and 1 strand of B, pick up and knit 60 sts evenly along cast-on cuff-top edge on one sock, working into the inner loops of the cast-on sts when picking up sts and distributing sts over 3 needles.

Place a stitch marker on needle at beg of round (slipping it when reached throughout), then using 4th needle to knit with, beg frill as follows:

Round 1 (WS) P to end.

Round 2 P to end.

Round 3 P into front and back of each st. *120 sts.*

Rep last 2 rounds once more. *240 sts.*

Bind off loosely purlwise.

Turn sock right side out.

Work inner frill on other sock in exactly same way.

TO FINISH SOCKS

Weave in any yarn ends.

Press very lightly on the wrong side, avoiding the frill and referring to the yarn label for the pressing instructions. (See page 116.)

gift bag

TO MAKE GIFT BAG

Using size 1 (2.5mm) double-pointed needles and AB, cast on 9 sts (leaving a tail of yarn about 8in/20cm long) with thumb or cable cast-on and distribute these sts over 3 needles, placing 3 sts on each needle (see page 48). Making sure cast-on sts are not twisted, hold 3 needles in a ring ready to beg first round and place a stitch

knitting in the round with four needles

Follow these simple steps for knitting in the round with a set of four double-pointed needles. Double-pointed needles are usually sold in sets of five. You can use three plus a working needle for small items as shown here, or four plus your working needle when you have more stitches. The first two or three rounds will be the hardest, and after that it all falls into place. Remember that when you work stockinette stitch in the round, you only work in knit stitch as you only ever work on the right side, round and round.

1 Cast on all the stitches required onto one of the needles. Then distribute the stitches evenly onto three of the double-pointed needles, leaving the fourth needle to knit with. Take care when moving the stitches along not to twist the work.

2 Hold the three needles with the stitches on them in a ring as shown, again making sure the stitches are not twisted.

3 Place a stitch marker on the right needle at end of the cast-on stitches—this is to mark the beginning/end of each row. (You can use a plastic stitch marker or simply make your own stitch marker by tying a little ring with a piece of contrasting cotton yarn.) Now insert the tip of the fourth needle into the first stitch on the left needle to join the work together and begin the first stitch of the first round. Continue to knit round and round, slipping the stitch marker each time you reach it.

1

2

3

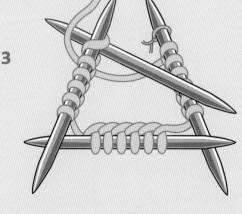

marker on right needle at end of cast-on sts to mark beg/end of round.

Using 4th needle to knit with and slipping marker when reached throughout, beg bag as follows:

Rounds 1 and 2 K to end.

Round 3 *K1, K into front and back of next st; rep from * to last st, K1. *13 sts.*

Round 4 K to end.

Round 5 Rep round 3.

Rounds 6 and 7 Rep rounds 4 and 5. *28 sts.*

Round 8 K to end.

Round 9 *K1, K into front and back of next st; rep from * to end. *42 sts.*

Round 10 K to end.

Round 11 *K2, K into front and back of next st; rep from * to end. *56 sts.*

Round 12 K to end.

Round 13 *K3, K into front and back of next st; rep from * to end. *70 sts.*

Round 14 K to end.

Round 15 *K6, K into front and back of next st; rep from * to end. *80 sts.*

Work even in St st (knit every round) until bag measures 6in/15cm from cast-on point.

Next round *K2, K2tog; rep from * to end. *60 sts.*

Knit 2 rounds.

Next round (eyelet round) *Yo, K2tog, K3; rep from * to end.

Knit 2 rounds.

Bind off knitwise.

OUTER AND INNER FRILLS

Work outer and inner frills on bag as for outer and inner frills on Socks, but picking up 60 sts along bound-off edge of bag.

TO FINISH GIFT BAG

Thread the long yarn tail at cast-on end of the bag onto a blunt-ended yarn sewing needle and weave it through the 9 cast-on sts, then pull the yarn to gather the stitches and close the opening. Secure the yarn end on the wrong side of the bag.

Weave in any remaining yarn ends.

Press the bag very lightly on the wrong side, avoiding the frills and referring to the yarn label for the pressing instructions. (See page 116.)

Thread the ribbon through the eyelets to form the drawstring. Then carefully fold the gorgeous socks up and pop into the bag!

mochachino boa

Big, bold and not skinny, this is a confection of frills and picot binding off. The finished boa is approximately 94¹/₂in (240cm) long and very lovely and fat. It is constructed lengthwise so the length of the boa is determined by the number of stitches you cast on.

Along the spine of the boa you knit three opulent frills in shades of brown. The froth along the edges is made by knitting a picot bind-off. I am not going to lie to you and say the bind-off is quick, because it's not. But the rhythm of this bind-off is very soothing, CD-book-listening knitting—and the result is worth the time and effort.

SKILL LEVEL
Easy

SIZE OF BOA
The finished boa measures approximately 94 1/2in/ 240cm long.

WHAT YOU NEED
Rowan *Kidsilk Aura* in three colors as follows:

A   4 x 7/8oz/25g balls in coffee (754 Antique Bronze)
B   3 x 7/8oz/25g balls in milk chocolate (759 Bark)
C   2 x 7/8oz/25g balls in cream (752 Wheat)
Size 8 (5mm) circular knitting needle, 32in/80cm or 39in/100cm long

GAUGE
There is no need to work this boa to a specific gauge. The final length will vary slightly from knitter to knitter, which won't matter at all.

ABBREVIATIONS
See page 116.

FIRST FRILL LAYER (coffee)
Using size 8 (5mm) circular needle and A, cast on 220 sts loosely, with thumb or cable cast-on method (see pages 76 and 95).
Working back and forth in rows on circular needle throughout and beg with a K row, work 4 rows in St st, ending with RS facing for next row.
Row 5 (RS) *K1, K into front and back of next st; rep from * to end. *330 sts.*
Row 6 P to end.
Row 7 Rep row 5. *495 sts.*
Row 8 P to end.
Row 9 *K1, K into front and back of next st; rep from * to last st, K1. *742 sts.*
Row 10 P to end.
Rows 11 Rep row 5. *1,113 sts.*

Rows 12 P to end.

Picot edging
Work the picot bind-off on RS as follows:
*Using lace cast-on method (see page 114), cast on 2 sts onto LH needle, bind off 4 sts knitwise, transfer st on RH needle back onto LH needle; rep from * to last st, bind off last st and fasten off.

SECOND FRILL LAYER (milk chocolate)
Hold First Frill Layer with WS facing and cast-on edge uppermost, then using size 8 (5mm) circular needle and B, pick up and knit 220 sts evenly all across cast-on edge (see page 88).
Beg with a K row, work 4 rows in St st, ending with RS facing for next row.
Row 5 (RS) *K1, K into front and back of next st; rep from * to end. *330 sts.*
Row 6 P to end.
Row 7 Rep row 5. *495 sts.*
Row 8 P to end.
Row 9 *K1, K into front and back of next st; rep from * to last st, K1. *742 sts.*
Row 10 P to end.

Picot edging
Work the picot bind-off on RS as follows:
*Using lace cast-on method, cast on 2 sts onto LH needle, bind off 4 sts, transfer st on RH needle back to LH needle; rep from * to end and fasten off.

INNER FRILL (cream)
With RS facing and using size 8 (5mm) circular knitting needle and C, pick up and knit 220 sts evenly along center join between First Frill Layer and Second Frill Layer.
Row 1 (RS) K into front and back of each st to end. *440 sts.*
Row 2 P to end.
Row 3 Rep row 1. *880 sts.*
Row 4 P to end.

Picot edging

Work the picot bind-off on RS
as follows:
*Using lace cast-on method,
cast on 2 sts onto LH needle,
bind off 4 sts, transfer st on RH
needle back to LH needle; rep
from * to end and fasten off.

TO FINISH BOA

Weave in any yarn ends. There
is no need to press.

st. ives pillow

The gorgeous fading in the pink stripes of this knitted pillow cover is achieved by exploiting one of the most endearing qualities of Rowan *Kidsilk Haze*: its ability to fade in and out of shades and to create a whole new palette if you use different shades held together. The pillow front is knitted with two strands held together throughout, so when I wanted the light pink to fade into the darker wine red, I used one strand of each shade for two rows. You can achieve the same effect with many of the shades of *Kidsilk Haze*.

To contrast with the hazy, drifting colors on the front, I chose a crisp and contemporary Rowan fabric for the pillow back—Amy Butler's *Full Bloom* in Duck Egg from the Belle collection. The vibrant shades work well with the more muted mohair.

SKILL LEVEL
Easy

SIZE OF PILLOW
The finished pillow cover measures approximately 18in/46cm square.

WHAT YOU NEED
Rowan *Kidsilk Haze* in three colors as follows:

A   1 x 7/8oz/25g ball in pale blue-green (640 Glacier)

B   1 x 7/8oz/25g ball in light rose pink (583 Blushes)

C   1 x 7/8oz/25g ball in wine red (595 Liqueur)

Pair of size 5 (3.75mm) knitting needles

For a two-piece fabric backing, piece of cotton fabric 19in/49cm x 27in/70cm and a large snap; *or* for a one-piece backing, piece of cotton fabric 19in/49cm square

Matching sewing thread for backing

Pillow form to fit finished cover

GAUGE
25 sts and 32 rows to 4in/10cm square measured over St st using two strands of yarn held together and size 5 (3.75mm) needles *or needle size necessary to obtain correct gauge.*

ABBREVIATIONS
See page 116.

SPECIAL PATTERN NOTE
The pillow cover is worked with two strands of yarn held together throughout. The colors are mixed together, so sometimes two strands of the same color are used together, and sometimes one strand each of two different colors are used together. The colors used are abbreviated as follows:

If the patterns calls for AA, use 2 strands of A held together; if it calls for BB, use 2 strands of B held together; if it calls for BC, use 1 strand of B and 1 strand of C held together; and so on.

PILLOW COVER FRONT
Using size 5 (3.75mm) needles and AA (see Special Pattern Note above), cast on 115 sts with thumb or cable cast-on method (see pages 76 and 95).

Beg with a K row (and cutting off and joining in strands as required), work in St st in stripes as follows:

Work 10 rows in AA.

Work 3 rows in BB.

Work 2 rows in BC.

Work 3 rows in CC, so ending with RS facing for next row.

(This 18-row stripe sequence is repeated to form St st stripe patt.)

Cont in St st stripe patt until pillow cover front measures 18in/46cm from cast-on edge, ending

Alison's tips

• When you are using two strands of the same color yarn, roll half the ball off into a second ball, rather than taking one end from the inside and one from the outside of the ball. Taking from the inside of Rowan *Kidsilk Haze* can make a bit of a rat's nest of the yarn!

• You can choose whatever fabric and shades of yarn you like for your pillow cover. Or knit the back instead of using fabric for it. You could match a knitted back to the front or use one of the yarn shades on its own. See how much yarn you have left over from the front and then buy more yarn for the back accordingly.

with RS facing for bind-off.
Bind off knitwise.

TO FINISH PILLOW COVER
Weave in any yarn ends.
Press the knitted front very lightly on the wrong side, referring to the yarn label for the pressing instructions. (See page 116.)

Pillow cover back
For a two-piece fabric backing, cut the fabric into two pieces, each 19in/49cm by 13$\frac{1}{2}$in/35cm. Turn under $\frac{1}{2}$in/1.5cm twice along one long edge of each piece and sew these double hems. With right sides together, sew the two pieces to the knitted front so that the hemmed edges overlap at the center, taking a $\frac{1}{2}$in/1.5cm seam allowance on the fabric and stitching close to the edge on the knitting. Turn right side out. Sew on a large snap to close the back. Insert the pillow form.

Alternatively, for a one-piece fabric backing, cut a piece of fabric to the same size as the finished knitted front, plus an extra $\frac{1}{2}$in/1.5cm all around the edge for the seam allowance. With the right sides facing, sew the fabric back to the knitted front along three sides, taking a $\frac{1}{2}$in/1.5cm seam allowance on the fabric and stitching close to the edge on the knitting. Turn the cover right side out, insert the pillow form, and sew the last side closed.

wedding mittens and gift bag

Knitted in cream using two strands of yarn, these Rowan *Kidsilk Haze* mittens are so delicate. They are even suitable for a frosty winter wedding day. A subtle touch is the addition of pearly beads to the delicate frills.

If the bride has attendants, their mittens could be knitted in shades to match their wedding outfits, too. They can easily be scaled down for tiny hands. I also thought that the small gift bags would be a lovely way for little bridesmaids to carry dried flower petals or confetti for sprinkling the happy couple with after the ceremony!

SKILL LEVEL
Intermediate

SIZE OF MITTENS AND GIFT BAG
Mittens: The mittens can be worked in two different women's sizes—*small to medium* and *medium to large*; to fit palm circumferences 6¹/₂–7in/17–18cm and 7–7¹/₂in/18–19cm. The figures for the smallest size are given first in the instructions and the figures for the largest size follow in parentheses; where there is only one set of figures, it applies to both sizes. You can adjust the length of the mittens by adding to or subtracting from the number of rounds.
Gift bag: The finished bag measures approximately 4in/10cm wide by 4¹/₂in/11.5cm tall, excluding frills.

WHAT YOU NEED
2 x ⁷/₈oz/25g balls of Rowan *Kidsilk Haze* in white (634 Cream)
Set of four size 2 (2.75mm) double-pointed knitting needles
1 stitch holder
3 stitch markers
Approximately 173 crystal 3mm glass beads (Rowan ref: small clear bead J3001007)
28in/70cm of ⁵/₈in/1.5cm wide ribbon, for gift bag

Alison's tip

• If you decide to knit the optional double frill around the wrist and intend to make the gift bag as well, you'll probably need more yarn—so buy an extra ball just in case.

GAUGE
34 sts and 39 rows to 4in/10cm square measured over St st using two strands of yarn held together and size 2 (2.75mm) needles *or needle size necessary to obtain correct gauge.*

ABBREVIATIONS
bead 1 = bring yarn to RS of work between the 2 needles, slide the bead up next to st just worked, slip next stitch purlwise from LH needle to RH needle, then take yarn back to WS of work between the 2 needles, leaving bead sitting on RS of work in front of slipped st. *See also page 116.*

SPECIAL PATTERN NOTES
The mittens are made using two strands of yarn held together throughout, but the beaded frills are made using a single strand of yarn.
See page 23 for how to thread beads easily onto yarn.

mittens

TO MAKE MITTENS (make 2)
Using size 2 (2.75mm) double-pointed needles and 2 strands of yarn held tog, cast on 50 (56) sts and distribute these sts over 3 needles—placing 17 (19) sts on each of the first 2 needles and 16 (18) sts on the 3rd needle (see page 48).
Making sure cast-on sts are not twisted, hold 3 needles in a ring ready to beg first round and place a stitch marker on right needle at end of cast-on sts to mark beg/end of round.
Using 4th needle to knit with, beg cuff ribbing as follows:
Round 1 (RS) *K1, P1; rep from * to end of round.
(Last round is repeated to form single rib.)
Cont in rib as set (slipping marker when reached) until cuff measures 2¹/₄in/6cm from cast-on edge.
Work in St st (knit every round) for ¹/₂in/1cm.

Thumb gusset

Cont to slip st marker at beg of round when reached throughout, beg shaping thumb gusset as follows:

Next round K20 (26), place first gusset marker, M1, K1, M1, place second gusset marker, K29.

Next round K to end, slipping markers when reached.

Next round K20 (26), slip marker, M1, K3, M1, slip marker, K29.

Next round K to end, slipping markers when reached.

Next round K20 (26), slip marker, M1, K5, M1, slip marker, K29.

Next round K to end, slipping markers when reached.

Cont in this way, slipping all markers when reached and inc 1 st at each side of thumb gusset on next round and every foll alt round until there are a total of 19 sts between two gusset markers.

Knit 1 round.

Next round K20 (26), place next 19 sts on a st holder (or on waste yarn or a large safety pin—you will return to these later for thumb) removing gusset markers, cast on 3 sts onto LH needle, then bunch up 19 sts on holder in order to reach across them and cont round, K to end of round. *52 (58) sts.*

Next round K19 (25), skp, K1, K2tog, K28. *50 (56) sts.*

(**Tip:** If you find a gap or a strand of yarn has appeared at the base of the thumb on the WS, pick up this strand on the following round and slip it onto LH needle, next K it and next st tog through the back loops.)

Knit 8 rounds. (You can work more or fewer rounds here to achieve 3/4in/2cm less than desired finished length.)

Work 3/4in/2cm in single rib as for cuff. Bind off in rib.

Thumb

With RS facing and using size 2 (2.75mm) double-pointed needles, distribute 19 sts on holder over 3 needles, then rejoin 2 strands of yarn held tog and pick up and knit 5 sts along 3 sts cast on at base of thumb. *24 sts.*

Using 4th needle to knit with, beg thumb ribbing as follows:

Next round (RS) Place marker to mark beg of round, K to last 5 sts, K2tog, K3, slip marker off, K2tog, replace marker. *22 sts.*

Work in single rib for 1/2–3/4in/1.5–2cm or as desired. Bind off in rib.

Make second mitten in exactly same way.

FINGER-OPENING OUTER FRILLS

Thread 30 (32) beads onto 1 strand of yarn before casting on with this yarn.

With RS facing and using size 2 (2.75mm) double-pointed needles and 1 strand of yarn, pick up and knit 44 (48) sts along bound-off edge of finger opening on one mitten (see page 88), working into the outer loops of the bound-off sts when picking up sts and distributing sts over 3 needles.

Place a stitch marker on needle at beg of round (slipping it when reached throughout), then using 4th needle to knit with, beg frill as follows:

Round 1 (RS) K into front and back of each st. *88 (96) sts.*

Round 2 K to end.

Round 3 Rep round 1. *176 (192) sts.*

Round 4 (beading round) *Bead 1, K5; rep from * to last 2 (6) sts, bead 1, K1 (5). *30 (32) beads placed.*

Bind off very loosely knitwise.

Work outer frill on other mitten in exactly same way.

FINGER-OPENING INNER FRILLS

Turn one mitten inside out and with WS facing and using size 2 (2.75mm) double-pointed needles and 1 strand of yarn, pick up and knit 44 (48) sts evenly along bound-off edge of finger opening on one mitten, working into the inner loops of the bound-off sts when picking up sts and distributing sts over 3 needles.

Place a stitch marker on needle at beg of round (slipping it when reached throughout), then using 4th needle to knit with, beg frill as follows:

Round 1 (WS) P to end.

Round 2 P into front and back of each st. *88 (96) sts.*

Round 3 P to end.
Round 4 Rep round 2. *176 (192) sts.*
Bind off very loosely purlwise.
Turn mitten right side out.
Work inner frill on other mitten in exactly same way.

OUTER AND INNER WRIST FRILLS (optional)
If you wish, work a double frill around wrist cuff of
mittens, following instructions for finger-opening frills
but picking up stitches around cast-on edge.

TO FINISH MITTENS
Weave in any yarn ends, using the loose ends at the base
of the thumb to close any gap there.
Press very lightly on the wrong side, avoiding the frill and
referring to the yarn label for the pressing instructions.
(See page 116.)

gift bag

TO MAKE GIFT BAG
Using size 2 (2.75mm) double-pointed needles and
2 strands of yarn held tog, cast on 9 sts (leaving a tail of
yarn about 8in/20cm long) and distribute these sts over
3 needles, placing 3 sts on each needle (see page 48).
Making sure cast-on sts are not twisted, hold 3 needles
in a ring ready to beg first round and place a stitch
marker on right needle at end of cast-on sts to mark
beg/end of round.
Using 4th needle to knit with and slipping marker when
reached throughout, beg bag as follows:
Rounds 1 and 2 K to end.
Round 3 *K1, K into front and back of next st; rep from *
to last st, K1. *13 sts.*
Round 4 K to end.
Round 5 Rep round 3.
Rounds 6 and 7 Rep rounds 4 and 5. *28 sts.*
Round 8 K to end.

Round 9 *K1, K into front and back of next st; rep from *
to end. *42 sts.*
Round 10 K to end.
Round 11 *K2, K into front and back of next st; rep from
* to end. *56 sts.*
Round 12 K to end.
Round 13 *K3, K into front and back of next st; rep from
* to end. *70 sts.*
Work even in St st (knit every round) until bag measures
3 1/2in/9cm from cast-on point.
Next round K to end.
Next round *K5, K2tog; rep from * to end. *60 sts.*
Knit 2 rounds.
Next round (eyelet round) *Yo, K2tog, K3; rep from *
to end.
Knit 2 rounds.
Bind off knitwise.

OUTER FRILL
Thread 45 beads onto 1 strand of yarn before casting on
with this yarn.
With RS facing and using size 2 (2.75mm) double-
pointed needles and 1 strand of yarn, pick up and knit
56 sts evenly along bound-off edge of bag (see page 88),
working into the outer loops of the bound-off sts when
picking up sts and distributing sts over 3 needles.
Place a stitch marker on needle at beg of round (slipping
it when reached throughout), then using 4th needle to
knit with, beg frill as follows:
Round 1 (RS) K into front and back of each st. *112 sts.*
Round 2 K to end.
Round 3 Rep round 1. *224 sts.*
Round 4 (beading round) *K4, bead 1; rep from * last
4 sts, K3, bead 1, K1. *45 beads placed.*
Bind off very loosely knitwise.

INNER FRILL
Turn bag inside out and with WS facing and using size 2
(2.75mm) double-pointed needles and 1 strand of yarn,

pick up and knit 56 sts evenly along bound-off edge of bag, working into the inner loops of the bound-off sts when picking up sts and distributing sts over 3 needles.

Place a stitch marker on needle at beg of round (slipping it when reached throughout), then using 4th needle to knit with, beg frill as follows:

Rounds 1 and 2 (WS) P to end.

Round 3 P into front and back of each st. *112 sts*.

Round 4 P to end.

Round 5 Rep round 3. *224 sts*.
Bind off very loosely purlwise.
Turn bag right side out.

TO FINISH GIFT BAG

Thread the long yarn tail at cast-on end of the bag onto a blunt-ended yarn sewing needle and weave it through the 9 cast-on sts, then pull the yarn to gather the stitches and close the opening. Secure the yarn end on the wrong side of the bag.

Weave in any remaining yarn ends.

Press the bag very lightly on the wrong side, avoiding the frills and referring to the yarn label for the pressing instructions. (See page 116.)

Thread the ribbon through the eyelets to form the drawstring.

flower trellis scarf

This is an example of how obliging Rowan *Kidsilk Haze* is when teamed with other Rowan yarns. Cotton-mix Rowan *Calmer* offers a beautiful contrast to *Kidsilk Haze*, being everything *Kidsilk Haze* is not. *Calmer* is mat, completely smooth, round, generously proportioned for fast-growing knitting, and has slight stretch. Combine this equable temperament with the frothy and excitable mohair for a very happy combination.

The base trellis is easy and fast to knit, whereupon you can have fun with the flowers and leaves. Scatter them across both ends of the scarf, leaving the center two thirds of the scarf free of foliage.

SKILL LEVEL
Intermediate

SIZE OF SCARF
The finished scarf measures approximately 7¼in/18cm wide by 52in/132cm long.

WHAT YOU NEED
A 2 x 1¾oz/50g balls of Rowan *Calmer* in dusty green (474 Khaki)

B 1 x ⅞oz/25g ball of Rowan *Kidsilk Haze* in hot pink (606 Candy Girl)

C 1 x ⅞oz/25g ball of Rowan *Kidsilk Haze* in lime green (597 Jelly)

D 1 x ⅞oz/25g ball of Rowan *Kidsilk Haze* in burgundy (595 Liqueur)

Pair of size 9 (5.5mm) knitting needles

1 stitch holder

Approximately 266 crystal 3mm glass beads (Rowan ref: small clear bead J3001007)

Sewing thread in a color to match yarn A, for sewing foliage to scarf

Alison's tip

• I used a vibrant and irresistible pink and the vivid acid green for the leaves, but you can easily vary the mood all together by being more subdued and subtle than me! The flowers and leaves make good "travel knitting" if you use short needles, and this also breaks up the slight tedium of knitting a whole bouquet at one time.

GAUGE
23 sts and 26 rows to 4in/10cm square measured over trellis pattern using A and size 9 (5.5mm) needles *or needle size necessary to obtain correct gauge.*

ABBREVIATIONS
bead 1 = bring yarn to RS of work between the 2 needles, slide the bead up next to st just worked, slip next stitch purlwise from LH needle to RH needle, then take yarn back to WS of work between the 2 needles, leaving bead sitting on RS of work in front of slipped st.
See also page 116.

SPECIAL PATTERN NOTES
The stitch pattern causes the ends of the trellis to slope; this is on purpose, so do not be alarmed.

For tips on how to thread beads easily onto yarn, turn to page 23.

TO MAKE SCARF
Using size 9 (5.5mm) needles and A, cast on 42 sts loosely with thumb cast-on method (see page 76).
Row 1 (RS) K to end.
Row 2 Sl 1 knitwise, K to end.
Beg trellis patt as follows:
Row 3 Sl 1 knitwise, K1, *yo, K2tog; rep from * to last 2 sts, K2.
Row 4 Sl 1 knitwise, K1, P to last 2 sts, K2.
(Rows 3 and 4 are repeated to form trellis patt.)
Rep rows 3 and 4 until almost all the yarn is used up, ending with a *row 4* and retaining just enough yarn to knit the 2 final rows and work bind-off.
Next 2 rows Sl 1 knitwise, K to end.
Bind off knitwise.

LEAVES IN PAIRS (make 10 pairs)
Thread 2 beads onto yarn C before beginning each pair of leaves.

First leaf

Using size 9 (5.5mm) needles and C, cast on 3 sts with lace cast-on method (see page 114).

Row 1 (RS) K1, bead 1, K1.

Row 2 and all WS rows P to end.

Row 3 K into front and back of first st, k to last st, K into front and back of last st. *5 sts.*

Row 5 Rep row 3. *7 sts.*

Row 7 Rep row 3. *9 sts.*

Row 9 K2tog, K to last 2 sts, k2tog. *7 sts.*

Row 11 Rep row 9. *5 sts.*

Row 13 K2tog, K1, k2tog. *3 sts.***

Cut off yarn and slip these 3 sts onto a stitch holder.

Second leaf

Using size 9 (5.5mm) needles and C, cast on 3 sts with the lace cast-on method.

Work as for First Leaf to **.

Join second and first leaves

Join leaves together on next row as follows:

With WS facing, K first 2 sts of second leaf tog, K last st of Second Leaf tog with first st of First Leaf (on stitch holder), K last 2 sts of first leaf tog. *3 sts.*

Next row K3.

Next row K3tog and fasten off.

Make 9 more pairs of leaves in same way.

SINGLE-TIER FLOWERS (make 27)

Thread 8 beads onto yarn before beginning each flower. Using size 9 (5.5mm) needles and B, cast on 60 sts with lace cast-on method (see page 114).

Row 1 (RS) K1, bead 1, *K7, bead 1; rep from * to end last 2 sts, K2.

Row 2 K to end.

Row 3 K1, *skp; rep from * to last st, K1. *31 sts.*

Row 4 K1, *skp; rep from * to end. *16 sts.*

Do not bind off.

Cut off yarn, leaving a 8in/20cm long yarn tail, thread this yarn tail onto a blunt-ended sewing needle, and thread tail back through 16 sts on knitting needle,

slipping sts off knitting needle as you proceed. Pull yarn end to gather sts and form a rosette shape, then weave it in on WS of rosette to secure.

Make 13 more single-tier flowers using B (for a total of 14 in B).

Then make 13 in same way using D.

Reserve 3 single-tier flowers in B (bright pink) and 4 single-tier flowers in D (burgundy) to sew to the scarf as they are, and use the remaining 11 flowers in B and 9 flowers in D to make the double-tier flowers.

DOUBLE-TIER FLOWERS (make 10)

Make a total of 5 one-color double-tier flowers by laying 2 single-tier flowers on top of each other and stitching them together—use yarn B layers (bright pink) for 3 of the one-color flowers and yarn D (burgundy) layers for the remaining 2 one-color flowers.

Then make 5 two-color double-tier flowers, layering a bright pink single-tier flower on top of a burgundy one. Sew three beads to the center of each of the 10 double-tier flowers.

TO FINISH SCARF

Weave in any yarn ends on scarf and flowers.

Press the scarf very lightly on the wrong side, referring to the yarn label for the pressing instructions. (See page 116.)

Arrange four single-tier flowers and five double-tier flowers in place at one end of the scarf and three single-tier flowers and five double-tier flowers in place at the other end, trailing up toward the center—leave the center two thirds of the scarf without foliage. Then arrange five pairs of leaves at each end, under some of the flowers.

Using a sewing thread that matches yarn A, sew the flowers and foliage in place.

gathering scarf

Very delicate and floatly, this scarf uses only one ball of Rowan *Kidsilk Haze*, and once you have the pattern mastered, it takes only about a weekend to knit. It is lightly beaded and knitted up on oversized needles. The instructions for "gathering" of groups of stitches are easy to follow, and this stitch pattern makes the cast-on and bound-off edges form gentle scallops.

The lace texture is very obliging and looks equally pretty if you prefer a tighter knit for your scarf, which you can achieve by using size 6 (4mm) needles. Or, by extending the number of pattern repeats, you could easily make this a wider throw or a wrap that would be delightful for evening wear.

SKILL LEVEL
Intermediate

SIZE OF SCARF
The finished scarf measures approximately 9³/₄in/24.5cm wide by 50¹/₂in/126cm long, when laying flat and unstretched.

WHAT YOU NEED
Blue-green scarf
1 x ⁷/₈oz/25g ball of Rowan *Kidsilk Haze* in dark blue-green (582 Trance)
Pair of size 10¹/₂ (6.5mm) knitting needles
Approximately 200 crystal 4mm glass beads (Rowan ref: large clear bead J3001008)

Gold-brown scarf
1 x ⁷/₈oz/25g ball of Rowan *Kidsilk Haze* in gold-brown (626 Putty)
Pair of size 10¹/₂ (6.5mm) knitting needles
Approximately 200 bronze 3mm bronze glass beads in (Rowan ref bronze bead J3001009)

GAUGE
17¹/₂ sts and 19 rows to 4in/10cm square measured over "gathering" pattern using size 10¹/₂ (6.5mm) needles *or needle size necessary to obtain correct gauge.*

ABBREVIATIONS
bead 1 = bring yarn to RS of work between the 2 needles, slide the bead up next to st just worked, slip next stitch purlwise from LH needle to RH needle, then take yarn back to WS of work between the 2 needles, leaving bead sitting on RS of work in front of slipped st. *See also page 116.*

SPECIAL PATTERN NOTES
The number of stitches (43) in each row never alters. For tips on how to thread beads easily onto yarn, turn to page 23.

TO MAKE SCARF
Thread all the beads onto the yarn before beginning the scarf.
Using size 10¹/₂ (6.5mm) needles (and your chosen color), cast on 43 sts with lace cast-on method (see page 114).
Row 1 (RS) *K1tbl, K6, bead 1, K6; rep from * to last st, K1tbl.
Row 2 *P1tbl, P13; rep from * to last st, P1tbl.
Row 3 *K1tbl, K4tog, [yo, K1] 5 times, yo, K4togtbl; rep from * to last st, K1tbl.
Row 4 Rep row 2.
(These last 4 rows are repeated to form "gathering" patt.)
Rep rows 1–4 until almost all the yarn is used up, ending with a row 4 and retaining just enough yarn to bind off. Bind off loosely knitwise, trying to match looseness of bound-off edge to that of cast-on edge.

Alison's tips

• If working this lace pattern combined with working in Rowan *Kidsilk Haze* seems a bit daunting, work a few repeats in Rowan *4-Ply Cotton* on size 10¹/₂ (6.5mm) needles first to practice.

• When working the K4tog and the K4togtbl instructions, help yourself by being careful not to knit the rows before too tightly and by giving the four stitches a firm but gentle tug downward before you work the stitch.

TO FINISH SCARF

Weave in any yarn ends.
Before pressing, pin out the
scallop shapes at each end
firmly—they are more
pronounced at the cast-on
end, so try and get the ends
to match more closely at
both ends.

Then press the scarf very lightly
on the wrong side, referring to
the yarn label for the pressing
instructions. (See page 116.)

stella shrug

This colorwash shrug is knitted from cuff to cuff—in the round for the sleeves, but for the back section, it goes onto single-pointed needles to form the opening. The slightly flared sleeves are finished with a discreet row of crochet, embellished with triple-clusters of tiny bronze beads. Bonus: no seams! It snugly keeps the chill off your arms and back, and looks very flattering over a close-fitted T-shirt.

The Rowan *Kidsilk Haze* is held double throughout, and you drop and add shades to get the blended stripe effect. I used only five shades of yarn in pinks and grays, but, in fact, you get nine distinct color sections because of the yarn mixing in the pattern.

SKILL LEVEL
Intermediate

SIZE OF SHRUG
The finished shrug measures approximately 57in/142.5cm from cuff to cuff, but when worn stretches to approximately 59in/150cm from cuff to cuff.

WHAT YOU NEED
Rowan *Kidsilk Haze* in five colors as follows:
A 1 x ⁷/₈oz/25g ball in hot pink (606 Candy Girl)
B 1 x ⁷/₈oz/25g ball in wine red (595 Liqueur)
C 1 x ⁷/₈oz/25g ball in light rose pink (583 Blushes)
D 1 x ⁷/₈oz/25g ball in lavender-gray (589 Majestic)
E 1 x ⁷/₈oz/25g ball in gray (605 Smoke)
Set of four size 6 (4mm) double-pointed knitting needles
Size 6 (4mm) circular knitting needle
Approximately 174 bronze 3mm glass beads (Rowan ref: bronze bead J3001009)
Size G-6 (4mm) crochet hook
1 stitch marker

Alison's tip

• The finished garment is 59in (150cm) long from cuff to cuff, but you can easily adjust the length by working either more or fewer rows on the straight knitted back section. Alternatively, you can work more or fewer rounds in the colorwash knitted in-the-round sleeve sections, but if you do, make sure you work both sleeves the same. Measure yourself from wrist to wrist and across your upper back to find your personal number.

GAUGE
22 sts and 26 rows to 4in/10cm square measured over St st using two strands of yarn and size 6 (4mm) needles *or needle size necessary to obtain correct gauge.*

ABBREVIATIONS
See page 116.

SPECIAL PATTERN NOTES
Beads are used on the crocheted edging on this shrug. See page 23 for how to thread beads easily onto yarn. The shrug is worked with two strands of yarn held together throughout. The colors are mixed together, so sometimes two strands of the same color are used together, and sometimes one strand each of two different colors are used together. The colors used are abbreviated as follows:
If the patterns calls for AA, use 2 strands of A held together; if it calls for BB, use 2 strands of B held together; if it calls for BC, use 1 strand of B and 1 strand of C held together; and so on.

TO MAKE SHRUG
The shrug is worked from cuff to cuff, beginning with the cuff at one end of the shrug—the first sleeve is worked in the round, the back is then worked back and forth in rows, then the second sleeve is worked in the round.
First sleeve
Using size 6 (4mm) double-pointed needles and AA (see Special Pattern Note above), cast on 90 sts loosely, with thumb or cable cast-on method (see pages 76 and 95), and distribute these sts over 3 needles—placing 30 sts on each needle (see page 48).
Making sure cast-on sts are not twisted, hold 3 needles in a ring ready to beg first round and place a stitch marker on right needle at end of cast-on sts to mark beg/end of round.
Using 4th needle to knit with and AA (and slipping marker when reached throughout), beg cuff as follows:

Knit 3 rounds.

(Note: Because you are knitting in the round with RS always facing, knitting every round forms St st.)

Next round [K28, K2tog] 3 times. *87 sts.*

Knit 2 rounds.

Next round [K27, K2tog] 3 times. *84 sts.*

Knit 2 rounds.

Next round [K26, K2tog] 3 times. *81 sts.*

Knit 4 rounds.

Next round [K25, K2tog] 3 times. *78 sts.*

Change to AB and cont as follows:

Knit 4 rounds.

Next round [K24, K2tog] 3 times. *75 sts.*

Knit 15 rounds.

Cutting off and joining in strands as required, work in stripes as follows:

Knit 20 rounds in BB.

Knit 20 rounds in BC.

Knit 20 rounds in CC.

Knit 20 rounds in CD.

Knit 12 rounds in DD.

Back of shrug

Using size 6 (4mm) circular needle and removing stitch marker, purl all sts from double-pointed needles onto this single needle.

(Note: Changing from knitting in rounds to knitting in rows—where the sleeve opens out into the shrug back—will seem a little difficult at first, but try not to pull the knitting apart too much where the rows end and begin. This will quickly become easier as the opening widens.)

Working back and forth in rows on circular needle, cont in St st as follows:

Knit 1 row.

Purl 1 row.

Next row (RS) K3, M1, K to last 3 sts, M1, K3. *77 sts.*

Purl 1 row.

[Rep last 2 rows] once. *79 sts.*

Next row K3, M1, K to last 3 sts, M1, K3. *81 sts.*

Change to DE and cont as follows:

Purl 1 row.

Next row K3, M1, K to last 3 sts, M1, K3. *83 sts.*

[Rep last 2 rows] 5 times, so ending with WS facing for next row. *93 sts.*

Beg with a P row, 7 rows in St st, ending with RS facing for next row.

Change to EE and work in St st for 9³/4in/24.5cm, ending with RS facing for next row (you can adjust length of shrug across back here if desired).

Change to DE and work 8 rows, so ending with RS facing for next row.

Next row (RS) K3, skp, K to last 5 sts, K2tog, K3. *91 sts.*

Purl 1 row.

Next row K3, skp, K to last 5 sts, K2tog, K3. *89 sts.*

[Rep last 2 rows] 3 times. *83 sts.*

Purl 1 row.

Change to DD.

Next row K3, skp, K to last 5 sts, K2tog, K3. *81 sts.*

Purl 1 row.

[Rep last 2 rows] twice. *77 sts.*

Next row K3, skp, K to last 5 sts, K2tog, K3. *75 sts.*

Work 3 rows in St st, so ending with RS facing for next row.

Second sleeve

Using set of size 6 (4mm) double-pointed needles and placing stitch marker at beg of round, knit all sts from circular needle, distributing them on 3 of the double-pointed needles.

Using 4th needle to knit with and slipping marker when reached throughout, cont second sleeve as follows:

Knit 9 rounds.

Cutting off and joining in strands as required, work in stripes as follows:

Knit 20 rounds CD.

Knit 20 rounds in CC.

Knit 20 rounds in BC.

Knit 20 rounds in BB.

Knit 15 rounds AB.

Cont with AB, beg shaping as follows:

thumb cast-on method

The thumb cast-on, also called the single cast-on, is the easiest cast-on of all. Many of my patterns call for this cast-on or the cable cast-on (see page 95), as each creates a neat and even edge along the lower edge of the knitting. When my instructions say you can use either the thumb or cable cast-on, the choice is really up to you—use the one that you are the most comfortable with.

1 Make a slip knot as for any cast-on and place it on the right needle. Wrap the yarn coming from the ball around the back of your left thumb and hold it in the palm of your left hand as shown.

2 Insert the right needle from underneath into the loop around your left thumb.

3 Release the loop of yarn from your left thumb and gently pull the yarn to form the new loop on the right needle.

4 Wrap the yarn around your left thumb again and repeat steps 2 and 3 to make as many cast-on stitches as you need.

1
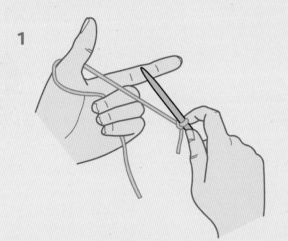

2
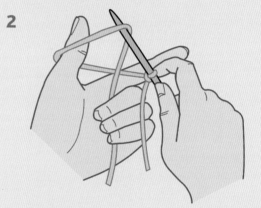

3
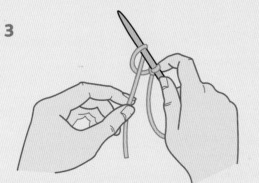

4

Next round [K25, M1] 3 times. *78 sts.*
Knit 4 rounds.

Change to AA and complete sleeve as
follows:

Next round [K26, M1] 3 times. *81 sts.*
Knit 4 rounds.

Next round [K27, M1] 3 times. *84 sts.*
Knit 2 rounds.

Next round [K28, M1] 3 times. *87 sts.*
Knit 2 rounds.

Next round [K29, M1] 3 times. *90 sts.*
Knit 3 rounds.

Bind off loosely knitwise.

CROCHET CUFF EDGING

Thread half the beads onto AA (2 strands
of A).

Turn shrug sleeves inside out and with WS
facing and using size G-6 (4mm) crochet
hook, join AA to one cuff edge and work
crochet edging evenly around cuff edge
as follows:

Round 1 (WS) Join AA with a slip stitch to
edge of cuff, ch 1, *1 sc, slide 3 beads up
close to RS of work, then keeping beads in
position, work 1 sc to complete beaded
cluster, ch 1, 1 sc, ch 1; rep from * to end
of round, join with a slip stitch to first sc
of round.

Fasten off.

Work crochet cuff edging on other cuff in
same way.

TO FINISH SHRUG

Weave in any yarn ends.

Press the shrug very lightly on the wrong
side, referring to the yarn label for the
pressing instructions. (See page 116.)

latticework scarf

This scarf is open and soft because of the Rowan *Kidsilk Haze*, yet drapey and substantial enough for a chilly evening because of the Rowan *4-Ply Cotton*. You hold one strand of each together and work the pattern on a large needle size to make the lacework open.

The two yarns really complement each other, and the smooth cotton makes the *Kidsilk Haze* very easy to work with as you knit this fairly simple lace scarf. The addition of the super-fine mohair yarn to the cotton yarn makes virtually no difference to the stitch size of the thicker yarn, and, in fact, you could add it to any other smoothly spun lightweight cotton or wool yarn and achieve a similar impact.

SKILL LEVEL
Advanced

SIZE OF SCARF
The finished scarf measures approximately 8¹/₂in/21cm wide by 65³/₄in/167cm long.

WHAT YOU NEED
A   3 x 1³/₄oz/50g balls of Rowan *4-Ply Cotton* in dusty purple (130 Ardour)
B   3 x ⁷/₈oz/25g balls of Rowan *Kidsilk Haze* in violet (600 Dewberry)
Pair of size 6 (4mm) knitting needles

GAUGE
24 sts and 28 rows to 4in/10cm square measured over lace pattern using one strand of A and one strand of B held together and size 6 (4mm) needles *or needle size necessary to obtain correct gauge.*

ABBREVIATIONS
See page 116.

SPECIAL PATTERN NOTE
Because the stitch count varies, if you want to check that you still have 51 stitches, only count stitches after rows 5, 6, and 11.

TO MAKE SCARF
Using size 6 (4mm) needles and 1 strand each of A and B held tog, cast on 51 sts loosely, with thumb cast-on method (see page 76).
Row 1 (RS) K1, *K2tog, K1, yo, K1, skp, K2; rep from * to last 2 sts, K2. *45 sts.*
Row 2 and all WS rows P to end.
Row 3 *K2tog, K1, [yo, K1] twice, skp; rep from * to last 3 sts, K3. *45 sts.*
Row 5 K2, *yo, K3, yo, K1, skp, K1; rep from * to last st, K1. *51 sts.*

Row 7 K4, *K2tog, K1, yo, K1, skp, K2; rep from * to last 7 sts, K2tog, K1, yo, K1, skp, K1. *45 sts.*
Row 9 K3, *K2tog, K1, [yo, K1] twice, skp; rep from * to end. *45 sts.*
Row 11 K2, *K2tog, K1, yo, K3, yo, K1; rep from * to last st, K1. *51 sts.*
Row 12 P to end.
(These last 12 rows are repeated to form lace patt.)
Cont in lace patt as set until scarf measures approximately 65³/₄in/167cm from cast-on edge, ending with a *row 11* so WS is facing for next row.
Bind off loosely purlwise, trying to match looseness of bound-off edge to that of cast-on edge.

TO FINISH SCARF
Weave in any yarn ends.
Press the scarf very lightly on the wrong side, referring to the yarn label for the pressing instructions. (See page 116.)

Alison's tip

• If you want to make this scarf wider so that it becomes a shawl, simply cast on more stitches. Just cast on a multiple of 6 stitches plus 3 extra stitches; for example, cast on 105 stitches for a 17¹/₂in (44cm) wide shawl. But don't forget to buy more yarn, especially if you want to make your shawl longer than the scarf!

sara mittens and gift bag

These mittens are feminine and very pretty. The mohair-only version, which blends two contrasting shades by using them held together, is more delicate; while the tweed and mohair version, though denser, is still fine and frilly.

The mittens can be worked in one of two sizes, and I think the smallest size will be best for most women. You can easily adjust the length of the mittens to your needs.

Because the tweed and mohair mittens are slightly thicker than the mohair ones, the single frill worked better. The mohair mittens look especially fun with a double frill around the finger opening and the wrist, but if you want a less frothy version, you can always omit the wrist frill.

SKILL LEVEL
Intermediate

SIZE OF MITTENS AND GIFT BAG
Mittens: The mittens can be worked in two different women's sizes—*small to medium* and *medium to large*; to fit palm circumferences 6^1/$_2$–7in/17–18cm and 7–7^1/$_2$in/18–19cm. The figures for the smallest size are given first in the instructions and the figures for the largest size follow in parentheses; where there is only one set of figures, it applies to both sizes. You can adjust the length of the mittens by adding to or subtracting from the number of rounds.

Gift bag: The finished gift bag measures approximately 4in/10cm wide by 4^1/$_2$in/11.5cm tall, excluding frills.

WHAT YOU NEED
Mohair mittens and mohair gift bag
A   2 x ^{7}/$_8$oz/25g balls of Rowan *Kidsilk Haze* in dark blue-green (582 Trance)

B   2 x ^{7}/$_8$oz/25g balls of Rowan *Kidsilk Haze* in lime green (597 Jelly)

Set of four size 2 (2.75mm) double-pointed knitting needles

28in/70cm of ^{5}/$_8$in/1.5cm wide ribbon, for gift bag

1 stitch holder

3 stitch markers

Tweed and mohair mittens
A   2 x ^{7}/$_8$oz/25g balls of Rowan *Scottish Tweed 4-Ply* in dark purple (016 Thistle)

B   1 x ^{7}/$_8$oz/25g ball of Rowan *Kidsilk Haze* in violet (600 Dewberry)

Set of four size 2 (2.75mm) double-pointed knitting needles

Set of four size 3 (3mm) double-pointed knitting needles

1 stitch holder

3 stitch markers

GAUGE
Mohair mittens and mohair gift bag: 34 sts and 39 rows to 4in/10cm square measured over St st using one strand of A and one strand of B held together and size 2 (2.75mm) needles *or needle size necessary to obtain correct gauge.*

Tweed and mohair mittens: 28 sts and 40 rows to 4in/10cm square measured over St st using one strand of A and one strand of B held together and size 3 (3mm) needles *or needle size necessary to obtain correct gauge.*

ABBREVIATIONS
See page 116.

SPECIAL PATTERN NOTE
The mittens and gift bag are worked with one strand of yarn A and one strand of yarn B held together throughout, but the frills are made using a single strand of yarn.

Alison's tips

• If you decide not to work the wrist frills on the Mohair Mittens, you will only need to buy one ball of each color and there will still be enough to make the bag!

• You can also knit in the round with a set of five double-pointed knitting needles instead of a set of four, and some knitters find this easier—you distribute the stitches over four needles and knit with the fifth. See page 48 for more about knitting in the round.

mohair mittens

TO MAKE MITTENS (make 2)

Using size 2 (2.75mm) double-pointed needles and 1 strand each of A and B held tog, cast on 50 (56) sts and distribute these sts over 3 needles—placing 17 (19) sts on each of the first 2 needles and 16 (18) sts on the 3rd needle (see page 48).

Making sure cast-on sts are not twisted, hold 3 needles in a ring ready to beg first round and place a stitch marker on right needle at end of cast-on sts to mark beg/end of round.

Using 4th needle to knit with, beg cuff ribbing as follows:

Round 1 (RS) *K1, P1; rep from * to end of round. (Last round is repeated to form single rib.)

Cont in rib as set (slipping marker when reached) until cuff measures 2¼in/6cm from cast-on edge.**

Work in St st (knit every round) for ½in/1cm.

Thumb gusset

Cont to slip st marker at beg of round when reached throughout, beg shaping thumb gusset as follows:

Next round K20 (26), place first gusset marker, M1, K1, M1, place second gusset marker, K29.

Next round K to end, slipping markers when reached.

Next round K20 (26), slip marker, M1, K3, M1, slip marker, K29.

Next round K to end, slipping markers when reached.

Next round K20 (26), slip marker, M1, K5, M1, slip marker, K29.

Next round K to end, slipping markers when reached.

Cont in this way, slipping all markers when reached and inc 1 st at each side of thumb gusset on next round and every foll alt round until there are a total of 19 sts between two gusset markers.

Knit 1 round.

Next round K20 (26), place next 19 sts on a st holder (or on waste yarn or a large safety pin—you will return to these later for thumb) removing gusset markers, cast on 3 sts onto LH needle, then bunch up 19 sts on

holder in order to reach across them and cont round, K to end of round. *52 (58) sts.*

Next round K19 (25), skp, K1, K2tog, K28. *50 (56) sts.*

(**Tip:** If you find a gap or a strand of yarn has appeared at the base of the thumb on the WS, pick up this strand on the following round and slip it onto LH needle, next K it and next st tog through the back loops.)

Knit 8 rounds. (You can work more or fewer rounds here to achieve ¾in/2cm less than desired finished length.)***

Work ¾in/2cm in single rib as for cuff.

Bind off in rib.

Thumb

With RS facing and using size 2 (2.75mm) double-pointed needles, distribute 19 sts on holder over 3 needles, then rejoin yarn (1 strand each of A and B held tog) and pick up and knit 5 sts along 3 sts cast on at base of thumb. *24 sts.*

Using 4th needle to knit with, beg thumb ribbing as follows:

Next round (RS) Place marker to mark beg of round, K to last 5 sts, K2tog, K3, slip marker off, K2tog, replace marker. *22 sts.*

Work in single rib for ½–¾in/1.5–2cm or as desired.

Bind off in rib.

Make second mitten in exactly same way.

FINGER-OPENING OUTER FRILLS

With RS facing and using size 2 (2.75mm) double-pointed needles and 1 strand of A, pick up and knit 44 (48) sts evenly along bound-off edge of finger opening on one mitten (see page 88), working into the outer loops of the bound-off sts when picking up sts and distributing sts over 3 needles.

Place a stitch marker on needle at beg of round (slipping it when reached throughout), then using 4th needle to knit with, beg frill as follows:

Round 1 (RS) K into front and back of each st. *88 (96) sts.*

Round 2 K to end.
Round 3 Rep round 1. *176 (192) sts.*
Bind off very loosely knitwise.
Work outer frill on other mitten in exactly same way.

FINGER-OPENING INNER FRILLS

Turn one mitten inside out and with WS facing and using size 2 (2.75mm) double-pointed needles and 1 strand of B, pick up and knit 44 (48) sts evenly along bound-off edge of finger opening on one mitten, working into the inner loops of the bound-off sts when picking up sts and distributing sts over 3 needles.

Place a stitch marker on needle at beg of round (slipping it when reached throughout), then using 4th needle to knit with, beg frill as follows:

Round 1 (WS) P to end.
Round 2 P into front and back of each st. *88 (96) sts.*
Round 3 P to end.
Round 4 Rep round 2. *176 (192) sts.*
Bind off very loosely purlwise.
Turn mitten right side out.
Work inner frill on other mitten in exactly same way.

OUTER AND INNER WRIST FRILLS

Work a double frill around wrist cuff of each mitten, following instructions for finger-opening frills, but picking up stitches evenly around cast-on edge.

TO FINISH MITTENS

Weave in any yarn ends, using the loose ends at the base of the thumb to close any gap there.

picking up stitches for frills

To make the many frills that feature in the book, I have used the technique of picking up stitches—a method you will already be familiar with if you have ever added a button band or collar to a knitted garment piece. Some of my frills are single, some are double or even triple.

In these steps the stitches are being picked up along the bound-off edge, but you may also need to pick up stitches along the cast-on edge or the side edge of the knitting, and the method for doing this is the same.

1 Hold the knitting with the right or wrong side facing as instructed. Then working from right to left along the edge of the knitting, insert the tip of the needle through the first bound-off loop. (The needle is shown here inserted under both loops of the bound-off stitch, but for the double frills along a bound-off edge you will be asked to pick up loops through one loop only of the bound-off stitch.)

2 Wrap the yarn being used for the frill around the tip of the needle as shown and pull the it through with the tip of the needle, just as if you are knitting a stitch through the bound-off loop.

3 This forms a loop on the needle. Insert the needle through the top of the next bound-off loop and pull the yarn through the next stitch in the same way.

4 Continue along the edge in this way, ensuring that you are picking up the stitches evenly along the edge.

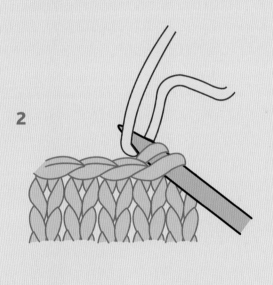

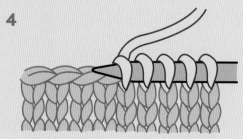

Press very lightly on the wrong side, avoiding the frill and referring to the yarn label for the pressing instructions. (See page 116.)

mohair gift bag

TO MAKE GIFT BAG

Using size 2 (2.75mm) double-pointed needles and 1 strand each of A and B held tog, cast on 9 sts (leaving a tail of yarn about 8in/20cm long) and distribute these sts over 3 needles, placing 3 sts on each needle (see page 48).

Making sure cast-on sts are not twisted, hold 3 needles in a ring ready to beg first round and place a stitch marker on right needle at end of cast-on sts to mark beg/end of round.

Using 4th needle to knit with and slipping marker when reached throughout, beg bag as follows:

Rounds 1 and 2 K to end.

Round 3 *K1, K into front and back of next st; rep from * to last st, K1. *13 sts.*

Round 4 K to end.

Round 5 Rep round 3.

Rounds 6 and 7 Rep rounds 4 and 5. *28 sts.*

Round 8 K to end.

Round 9 *K1, K into front and back of next st; rep from * to end. *42 sts.*

Round 10 K to end.

Round 11 *K2, K into front and back of next st; rep from * to end. *56 sts.*

Round 12 K to end.

Round 13 *K3, K into front and back of next st; rep from * to end. *70 sts.*

Work even in St st (knit every round) until bag measures 3^1/$_2$in/9cm from cast-on point.

Next round K to end.

Next round *K5, K2tog; rep from * to end. *60 sts.*

Knit 2 rounds.

Next round (eyelet round) *Yo, K2tog, K3; rep from * to end.

Knit 2 rounds.

Bind off knitwise.

OUTER FRILL

With RS facing and using size 2 (2.75mm) double-pointed needles and 1 strand of A, pick up and knit 50 sts evenly along bound-off edge of bag, working into the outer loops of the bound-off sts when picking up sts and distributing sts over 3 needles (see opposite page).

Place a stitch marker on needle at beg of round

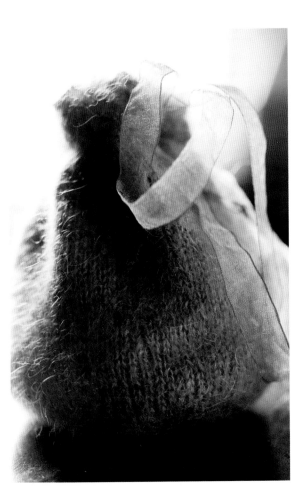

(slipping it when reached throughout), then using 4th needle to knit with, beg frill as follows:

Round 1 (RS) K into front and back of each st. *100 sts.*

Round 2 K to end.

Round 3 Rep round 1. *200 sts.*

Bind off very loosely knitwise.

INNER FRILL

Turn bag inside out and with WS facing and using size 2 (2.75mm) double-pointed needles and 1 strand of B, pick up and knit 50 sts evenly along bound-off edge of bag, working into the inner loops of the bound-off sts when picking up sts and distributing sts over 3 needles.

Place a stitch marker on needle at beg of round (slipping it when reached throughout), then using 4th needle to knit with, beg frill as follows:

Round 1 (WS) P to end.

Round 2 P into front and back of each st. *100 sts.*

Round 3 P to end.

Round 4 Rep round 2. *200 sts.*

Bind off very loosely purlwise.

Turn bag right side out.

TO FINISH GIFT BAG

Thread the long yarn tail at cast-on end of the bag onto a blunt-ended yarn sewing needle and weave it through the 9 cast-on sts, then pull the yarn to gather the stitches and close the opening. Secure the yarn end on the wrong side of the bag.

Weave in any remaining yarn ends.

Press the bag very lightly on the wrong side, avoiding the frills and referring to the yarn label for the pressing instructions. (See page 116.)

Thread the ribbon through the eyelets to form the drawstring.

tweed and mohair mittens

TO MAKE MITTENS (make 2)

Work as for Mohair Mittens to **.

Change to size 3 (3mm) double-pointed needles and cont as for Mohair Mittens to ***.

Change to size 2 (2.75mm) needles and complete as for Mohair Mittens.

FINGER-OPENING FRILLS

With RS facing and using size 3 (3mm) double-pointed needles and 1 strand of B, pick up and knit 44 (48) sts evenly along bound-off edge of finger opening on one mitten (see page 88), distributing sts over 3 needles.

Place a stitch marker on needle at beg of round (slipping it when reached throughout), then using 4th needle to knit with, beg frill as follows:

Round (RS) 1 K to end.

Round 2 K into front and back of each st. *88 (96) sts.*

Round 3 K to end.

Rep last 2 rounds. *176 (192) sts.*

Bind off loosely knitwise.

Work frill on other mitten in exactly same way.

TO FINISH MITTENS

Weave in any yarn ends, using the loose ends at the base of the thumb to close any gap there.

Press very lightly on the wrong side, avoiding the frill and referring to the yarn label for the pressing instructions. (See page 116.)

split-cable pillow

As Rowan *Kidsilk Aura* is a medium-weight mohair-mix yarn, it is ideal for cozy home accessories such as this pillow, which has a matching throw on page 96. I have backed the pillow with some lovely Amy Butler fabric (*Grandiflora* in Maroon from the Nigella range), but you can chose fabric that matches your own yarn color choice or knit a plain reverse stockinette stitch back.

The large split cable pattern set against a reverse stockinette stitch background is perfect for a medium-weight mohair; the yarn has the weight to form sculptural cables while retaining its lovely soft fuzz.

SKILL LEVEL
Intermediate to advanced

SIZE OF PILLOW
The finished pillow cover measures approximately 17³/4in/45cm square.

WHAT YOU NEED
5 x ⁷/8oz/25g balls of Rowan *Kidsilk Aura* in dusty rose (756 Raspberry)
Pair of size 8 (5mm) knitting needles
Cable needle
Piece of cotton fabric 18³/4in/48cm square, for pillow cover back, and matching sewing thread
Pillow form to fit finished cover

GAUGE
17 sts and 24 rows to 4in/10cm square measured over rev St st using size 8 (5mm) needles *or needle size necessary to obtain correct gauge.*

ABBREVIATIONS
C8B (cable 8 back) = slip next 4 sts onto cable needle and leave at back of work, K4 from LH needle, then K4 from cable needle.
C8F (cable 8 front) = slip next 4 sts onto cable needle and leave at front of work, K4 from LH needle, then K4 from cable needle.
See also page 116.

PILLOW COVER FRONT
Using size 8 (5mm) needles, cast on 104 sts with cable cast-on method (see opposite page) or thumb cast-on (see page 76).
Row 1 (RS) P20, [K16, P8] twice, K16, P20.
Row 2 and all WS rows K20, [P16, K8] twice, P16, K20.
Row 3 P20, [C8B, C8F, P8] twice, C8B, C8F, P20.
Row 5 Rep row 1.
Row 7 Rep row 3.

Row 9 Rep row 1.
Row 11 Rep row 1.
Row 13 P20, [C8F, C8B, P8] twice, C8F, C8B, P20.
Row 15 Rep row 1.
Row 17 Rep row 13.
Row 18 Rep row 2.
(These 18 rows are repeated to form cable patt.)
Cont in patt as set until front measures approximately 17³/4in/45cm from cast-on edge, ending with RS facing for bind-off and after a total of six 18-row repeats (a total of 108 rows) have been completed from cast-on edge.
Bind off in patt.

TO FINISH PILLOW COVER
Weave in any yarn ends.
Without squashing the cables, press the knitted front very lightly on the wrong side, referring to the yarn label for the pressing instructions. (See page 116.)
Pillow cover back
Cut a piece of fabric to the same size as the finished knitted front, plus an extra ¹/2in/1.5cm all around the edge for the seam allowance.
With the right sides facing, sew the fabric back to the knitted front along three sides, taking a ¹/2in/1.5cm seam allowance on the fabric and stitching close to the edge on the knitting. Turn the cover right side out, insert the pillow form and sew the last side closed.

cable cast-on method

The cable cast-on method gives you a firm edge with a line along the lower edge of the knitting. I often use this cast-on or the thumb cast-on (see page 76) when a neat, even, distinct edge is appropriate.

1 Make a slip knot as for any cast-on and place it on the left needle. Then knit into the slip knot and slip the new stitch back onto the left needle as for steps 1 and 2 of the lace cast-on (see page 114). Next, insert the right needle between the two stitches on the left needle as shown and knit a stitch through this space.

2 Insert the left needle into the resulting new stitch as shown by the arrow (from right to left through the front of the stitch) and slip it onto the left needle.

3 There are now three stitches on the left needle.

4 To make the following cast-on stitches, insert the right needle between the first two stitches on the left needle, and knit a stitch through this space. Again, transfer this stitch back onto the left needle. Repeat this step to make as many cast-on stitches as you need.

1
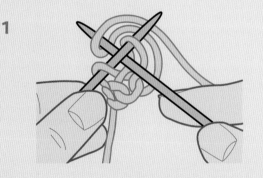

2
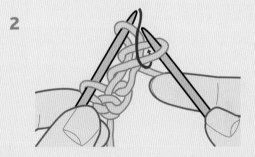

3
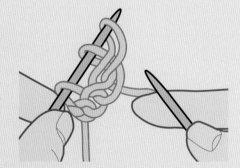

4
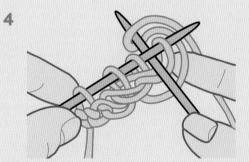

95

split-cable throw

Knitted to match the pillow on page 92, this throw is not huge but big enough to keep the chill off your knees as you sit and do a bit of autumn garden knitting. I am longing to make this in a bigger size and use some more of the Rowan *Kidsilk Aura* yummy shade palette. The pillow front's double split-cable pattern is widened here, so if you want a bigger throw, increase the repeats and just knit it longer.

If you sew you could easily back the throw with fabric to match the back of the pillow cover on page 92, maybe with some batting in between to create a mini lap-quilt.

SKILL LEVEL
Intermediate to advanced

SIZE OF THROW
The finished throw measures approximately 34¹/₄in/
87cm wide by 41¹/₂in/105cm long.

WHAT YOU NEED
13 x ⁷/₈oz/25g balls of Rowan *Kidsilk Aura* in dusty rose
(756 Raspberry)
Pair of size 8 (5mm) knitting needles
Cable needle

GAUGE
17 sts and 24 rows to 4in/10cm square measured over
rev St st using size 8 (5mm) needles *or needle size
necessary to obtain correct gauge.*

ABBREVIATIONS
C8B (cable 8 back) = slip next 4 sts onto cable needle
and leave at back of work, K4 from LH needle, then K4
from cable needle.
C8F (cable 8 front) = slip next 4 sts onto cable needle
and leave at front of work, K4 from LH needle, then K4
from cable needle.
See also page 116.

TO MAKE THROW
Using size 8 (5mm) needles, cast on 188 sts.
Row 1 (RS) P20, [K16, P8] twice, K16, P20, [K16, P8]
twice, K16, P20.
Row 2 and all WS rows K20, [P16, K8] twice, P16, K20,
[P16, K8] twice, P16, K20.
Row 3 P20, [C8B, C8F, P8] twice, C8B, C8F, P20, [C8B,
C8F, P8] twice, C8B, C8F, P20.
Row 5 Rep row 1.
Row 7 Rep row 3.
Row 9 Rep row 1.
Row 11 Rep row 1.

Row 13 P20, [C8F, C8B, P8] twice, C8F, C8B, P20, [C8F,
C8B, P8] twice, C8F, C8B, P20.
Row 15 Rep row 1.
Row 17 Rep row 13.
Row 18 Rep row 2.
(These 18 rows are repeated to form cable patt.)
Cont in patt as set until throw measures approximately
41¹/₂in/105cm from cast-on edge, ending with RS
facing for bind-off and after a total of fourteen 18-row
repeats (a total of 252 rows) have been completed from
cast-on edge.
Bind off in patt.

TO FINISH THROW
Weave in any yarn ends.
Without squashing the cables, press the throw very
lightly on the wrong side, referring to the yarn label for
the pressing instructions. (See page 116.)

Alison's tip

• Knitting cables with mohair yarn can be a
little tricky at first, because of the long
mohair fibers. If in doubt, practice with the
yarn before you start the throw. Cast on 24
stitches and knit four rows, working the first
and last 4 stitches in reverse stockinette
stitch and the center 8 stitches in stockinette
stitch. Then work one of the cables on the
next row over the center 8 stitches. Work a
few more rows without cables and bind off, or
repeat the cable a few times every fourth row.

lucia beaded wrap

Here is something simple enough to knit up quite quickly, yet with enough pattern content to keep your interest. This is an elegant two-tone stole or wrap, lightly beaded in pale gold to gently gleam away amidst the chocolate shades I have chosen.

 The crochet beaded border on the wrap is simplicity itself. Like any crochet I use, it has to be easy in order for me to conquer it—so I know that you can, too. Beaded crochet is even simpler than beaded knitting. I used single beads to decorate the crochet edges but there is no reason why you couldn't use clusters of three beads together on the edges, as I did with the edges on the shrug on page 72.

SKILL LEVEL
Advanced

SIZE OF WRAP
The finished wrap measures approximately 17³/₄in/
44.5cm wide by 65³/₄in/167cm long, including border.

WHAT YOU NEED
A 3 x ⁷/₈oz/25g balls of Rowan *Kidsilk Haze* in brown
(628 Cocoa)
B 1 x ⁷/₈oz/25g ball of Rowan *Kidsilk Haze* in gold-
brown (626 Putty)
Pair of size 5 (3.75mm) knitting needles
Size E-4 (3.5mm) crochet hook
Approximately 950 gold 3mm glass beads (Rowan ref:
gold bead J3001005)

GAUGE
23 sts and 27 rows to 4in/10cm square measured over
beaded lace pattern using size 5 (3.75mm) needles *or
needle size necessary to obtain correct gauge.*

ABBREVIATIONS
bead 1 = bring yarn to RS of work between the 2
needles, slide the bead up next to st just worked, slip
next stitch purlwise from LH needle to RH needle, then
take yarn back to WS of work between the 2 needles,
leaving bead sitting on RS of work in front of slipped st.
See also page 116.

SPECIAL PATTERN NOTE
For tips on how to thread beads easily onto yarn, turn to
page 23.

CENTER PANEL
Thread about one third of the beads onto each ball of
yarn A before beginning the ball. (After finishing the
center panel you will have more than enough beads left
for the crocheted border.)

Using size 5 (3.75mm) needles and A, cast on 84 sts
loosely, with the thumb cast-on method (see page 76).
Work 2 rows in garter st (knit every row).
Beg lace pattern as follows:
Row 1 (RS) K3, *bead 1, K7; rep from * to last 9 sts, bead
1, K8.
Rows 2 and 3 K to end.
Row 4 (WS) K2, P1, *yo, P2tog; rep from * to last 3 sts,
P1, K2.
Rows 5, 6 and 7 K to end.
Row 8 (WS) K2, P1, *P2tog, yo; rep from * to last 3 sts,
P1, K2.
Rows 9 and 10 K to end.
Row 11 *K7, bead 1; rep from * to last 4 sts, K4.
Rows 12 and 13 K to end.
Row 14 Rep row 4.
Rows 15, 16 and 17 K to end.
Row 18 Rep row 8.
(These 18 rows are repeated to form lace patt.)
Cont in lace patt as set until panel measures
approximately 62¹/₂in/159cm from cast-on edge, ending
with a *row 1* or a *row 11*.
Work 2 rows in garter st.
Bind off loosely knitwise, trying to match looseness of
bound-off edge to that of cast-on edge.

GARTER STITCH MITRED BORDER
With RS facing and using size 5 (3.75mm) needles and B,
pick up and knit 303 sts evenly along one long side edge
of Center Panel.
Row 1 (WS) K2, M1, K to last 2 sts, M1, K2.
Rep last row 10 times.
Bind off loosely knitwise.
Work a border along other long side edge in same way.
With RS facing and using size 5 (3.75mm) needles and B,
pick up and knit 83 sts evenly along cast-on edge of
Center Panel.
Row 1 (WS) K2, M1, K to last 2 sts, M1, K2.
Rep last row 10 times.

Bind off loosely knitwise.
Work a border along bound-off edge in same way.

BEADED CROCHET BORDER

Sew the mitred corner seams.

Thread remaining beads onto yarn A.

With WS facing and using size E-4 (3.5mm) crochet hook, join A to knitted border and work crochet border evenly around outer edge of wrap as follows:

Round 1 (WS) Join AA with a slip stitch to bound-off edge of knitted border, ch 1, *1 sc, slide 1 bead up close to RS of work, then keeping bead in position, work 1 sc to secure bead, ch 1, 1 sc, ch 1; rep from * to end of round, join with a slip stitch to first sc of round.

Fasten off.

TO FINISH WRAP

Weave in any yarn ends.

Press the scarf very lightly on the wrong side, referring to the yarn label for the pressing instructions. (See page 116.)

ribbed hat, scarf, and mittens

Here is a trio of really simple accessories in Rowan *Kidsilk Aura*.
The long-cuffed mittens offer an alternative to the *Kidsilk Haze*
mittens on page 82 (which are knitted in the round on double-
pointed needles). The ribbing is very easy, the work flows along
with speed and the finished items are very airy and light, but
super-snug and warm. Each is finished with a simple rosette
corsage or two, and a few beads.

The corsages on their own make super little gifts. If your lucky
gift-recipients don't merit a full three-piece set, you can whip up
the individual accessories in not much more than an evening's
knitting—present-giving problem solved.

SKILL LEVEL
Easy

SIZE OF HAT, SCARF, AND MITTENS
Hat: One size to fit women's average head size.
Scarf: Finished scarf measures approximately 8¼in/
20.5cm across widest point by 64½in/163cm long
Mittens: Women's size medium; to fit palm
circumference 7in/18cm.

WHAT YOU NEED
Hat with corsage
2 x ⁷/₈oz/25g balls of Rowan *Kidsilk Aura* in lavender
(757 Vintage)
Pair of size 4 (3.5mm) knitting needles
Pair of size 6 (4mm) knitting needles
Approximately 12 purple 6mm glass beads (GJ Beads ref:
SZ6-11212-9, Amethyst Lined Rose, size 6)
Scarf with corsages
5 x ⁷/₈oz/25g balls of Rowan *Kidsilk Aura* in lavender
(757 Vintage)
Pair of size 6 (4mm) knitting needles
Approximately 48 purple 6mm glass beads (GJ Beads ref:
SZ6-11212-9, Amethyst Lined Rose, size 6)
Mittens with corsages
2 x ⁷/₈oz/25g balls of Rowan *Kidsilk Aura* in lavender
(757 Vintage)
Pair of size 3 (3.25mm) knitting needles
Pair of size 5 (3.75mm) knitting needles
Approximately 24 purple 6mm glass beads (GJ Beads ref:
SZ6-11212-9, Amethyst Lined Rose, size 6)

GAUGE
Hat and scarf: 22 sts and 30 rows to 4in/10cm square
measured over rib pattern using size 6 (4mm) needles *or
needle size necessary to obtain correct gauge.*
Mittens: 22 sts and 29 rows to 4in/10cm square
measured over St st using size 5 (3.75mm) needles *or
needle size necessary to obtain correct gauge.*

ABBREVIATIONS
See page 116.

SPECIAL PATTERN NOTE
For tips on how to thread beads easily onto yarn, turn to
page 23.

hat

TO MAKE HAT
Using size 4 (3.5mm) needles, cast on 117 sts.
Row 1 (RS) *K1, P1; rep from * to last st, K1.
Row 2 P to end.
(These 2 rows are repeated to form rib patt.)
Cont in rib patt as set, until hat measures 2½in/6.5cm
from cast-on edge, ending with RS facing for next row.
Next row P to form foldline for brim foldback.
(The patt will now be reversed, so that the next row
becomes the RS of the work.)
Beg again with row 1 (RS) of rib patt (mark this side of
work as RS), cont in rib patt until hat measures 3½in/
9cm from cast-on edge.
Change to size 6 (4mm) needles.
Cont in patt until hat measures 8in/20cm from cast-on
edge, ending with RS facing for next row.
Shape hat
Change to St st and beg hat shaping as follows:
Next row (RS) *K2tog, K7; rep from * to end. *104 sts.*
Next row P to end.
Next row *K2tog, K6; rep from * to end. *91 sts.*
Next row P to end.
Next row *K2tog, K5; rep from * to end. *78 sts.*
Next row P to end.
Next row *K2tog, K4; rep from * to end. *65 sts.*
Next row P to end.
Next row *K2tog, K3; rep from * to end. *52 sts.*
Next row P to end.
Next row *K2tog, K2; rep from * to end. *39 sts.*

edge of the knitting to form the petal shapes, and gently pulling the yarn as you sew to draw up the knitted fabric into a pucker as you proceed.

Once the piece of knitting has been puckered, roll the corsage together to form a rosette and sew to secure shape. Using knitting yarn, sew four clusters of three beads each to the center of the corsage.

TO FINISH HAT

Weave in any yarn ends on the hat and the corsage. Do not press the corsage.

Press the hat very lightly on the wrong side, referring to the yarn label for the pressing instructions. (See page 116.)

Sew the hat seam, reversing the seam for 2¹/₂in/6.5cm from the cast-on edge for the folded back brim.

Sew or pin the corsage onto the folded back brim of the hat.

Next row P to end.
Next row *K2tog, K1; rep from * to end. *26 sts.*
Next row P to end.
Next row *K2tog; rep from * to end. *13 sts.*
Next row P to end.

Cut off yarn, leaving a long yarn tail, thread this yarn tail onto a blunt-ended sewing needle and thread tail back through 13 sts on knitting needle, slipping sts off knitting needle as you proceed. Pull yarn end to gather sts and secure.

CORSAGE

Using size 6 (4mm) needles, cast on 93 sts with lace cast-on method (see page 114).

Beg with a K row, work in St st for 4 rows.

Bind off loosely knitwise, leaving a long yarn tail.

Thread the tail onto a blunt-ending sewing needle and on the WS, work running stitch in zigzagging V's all along the bound-off edge, ensuring that the yarn goes over the

scarf

TO MAKE SCARF

Using size 6 (4mm) needles, cast on 5 sts.
Row 1 (RS) [K1, P1] twice, K1.
Row 2 P to end.
Row 3 Rep row 1.
Row 4 P1, P into front and back of next st, P to last 2 sts, P into front and back of next st, P1. *7 sts.*
Row 5 *P1, K1; rep from * to last st, P1.
Row 6 Rep row 4. *9 sts.*
Row 7 *K1, P1; rep from * to last st, K1.
Row 8 Rep row 4. *11 sts.*
[Rep rows 5–8] 8 times, then [rep rows 5 and 6] once. *45 sts.*
Next row *K1, P1; rep from * to last st, K1.
Next row P to end.
Next row *K1, P1; rep from * to last st, K1.
Rep last 2 rows until scarf measures 59in/150cm from

cast-on edge, ending with WS facing for next row.
Next row (WS) P1, P2tog, P to last 3 sts, P2tog, P1. *43 sts.*
Next row (RS) *P1, K1; rep from * to last st, P1.
Next row P1, P2tog, P to last 3 sts, P2tog, P1. *41 sts.*
Next row *K1, P1; rep from * to last st, K1.
Next row P1, P2tog, P to last 3 sts, P2tog, P1. *39 sts.*
[Rep last 4 rows] 8 times. *7 sts.*
Next row (RS) *P1, K1; rep from * to last st, P1.
Next row P1, P2tog, P1, P2tog, P1. 5 sts.
Next row [K1, P1] twice, K1.
Bind off purlwise.

CORSAGE (make 4)
Make 4 corsages as for Hat Corsage.

TO FINISH SCARF
Weave in any yarn ends on the scarf and the corsages.
Do not press the corsage.
Press the scarf very lightly on the wrong side, referring to the yarn label for the pressing instructions. (See page 116.)
Sew two corsages to each end of the scarf, placing them back to back.

mittens

TO MAKE MITTENS (make 2)
Using size 3 (3.25mm) needles, cast on 39 sts.
Row 1 (RS) *K1, P1; rep from * to last st, K1.

Row 2 P to end.

(These 2 rows are repeated to form rib patt.)

Cont in rib patt as set, until work measures 3in/7.5cm from cast-on edge, ending with RS facing for next row.

Change to size 5 (3.75mm) needles.

Beg with a K row, work in St st for 4in/10cm, ending with RS facing for next row.

Change to size 3 (3.25mm) needles.

Next row (RS) *K1, P1; rep from * to last st, K1.

Next row P to end.

Rep last 2 rows until rib patt measures 1¹/₂in/3.5cm, ending with WS facing for bind-off.

Bind off loosely purlwise.

Make second mitten in exactly same way.

FRILL

With RS facing and using size 3 (3.25mm) needles, pick up and knit 41 sts evenly along bound-off edge of one mitten (see page 88).

Row 1 (WS) P to end.

Row 2 K into front and back of each st to end. *82 sts.*

Rep last 2 rows. *164 sts.*

Purl 1 row.

Bind off loosely knitwise.

Work frill on second mitten in same way.

CORSAGE (make 2)

Make 2 corsages as for Hat Corsage.

TO FINISH MITTENS

Weave in any yarn ends on the mittens and the corsages. Do not press the corsage.

Press the mittens very lightly on the wrong side, avoiding the frill and referring to the yarn label for the pressing instructions. (See page 116.)

Fold each mitten in half with right sides facing and the side edges aligned, then sew the side seam, leaving a gap of the right length, and in the right place, for your thumb. Turn the mittens right side out.

Sew one corsage to back or cuff of each mitten.

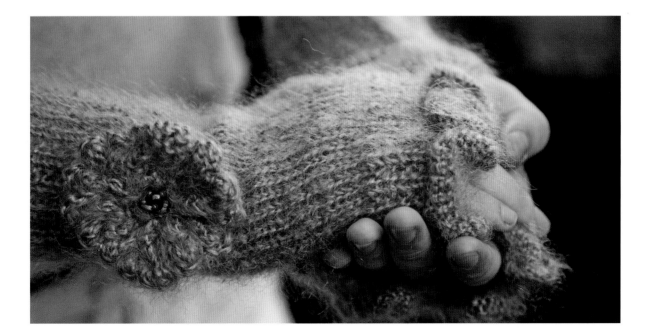

flower necklace, bracelet, and corsage

Here are patterns for two circles of flowers, one to adorn the neck and the other the wrist, and instructions for a corsage as well—made with a sturdy round cotton crochet base adorned with Rowan *Kidsilk Haze* loops all around the edge and filled with some more flowers in the middle.

The flowers are easy and quick to make. In fact, this is a great left-over-yarn-busting design, to use all the lovely fragments of mohair that you will have left over from some of the projects in this book.

Easy crochet in sturdy Rowan *4-Ply Cotton* provides a firm yet pretty "chain" for the necklace and bracelet—the crochet "chain" is then simply tied in place with narrow ribbon. Lovely.

SKILL LEVEL
Easy

SIZE OF NECKLACE, BRACELET, AND CORSAGE
Necklace and bracelet: The finished necklace and bracelet are tied on and the lengths can be adjusted to fit your needs.
Corsage: The finished corsage measures approximately 4 1/4in/11cm in diameter.

WHAT YOU NEED
A 1 x 7/8oz/25g ball of Rowan *Kidsilk Haze* in light cornflower blue (592 Heavenly)
B 1 x 7/8oz/25g ball of Rowan *Kidsilk Haze* in dark gray-blue (632 Hurricane)
C 1 x 1 3/4oz/50g of Rowan *4-Ply Cotton* in light blue (136 Bluebell)

Pair of size 3 (3.25mm) knitting needles
Size D-3 (3mm) crochet hook
Approximately 66 blue 6mm glass beads (GJ Beads ref: SZ6-312-9, Ocean Blue)
48in/120cm of 3/8in/1cm wide ribbon
Large safety pin or brooch-back, for corsage
Matching sewing thread for sewing beads, ribbon, and brooch-back in place

GAUGE
There is no need to work these accessories to a specific gauge.

ABBREVIATIONS
See page 116.

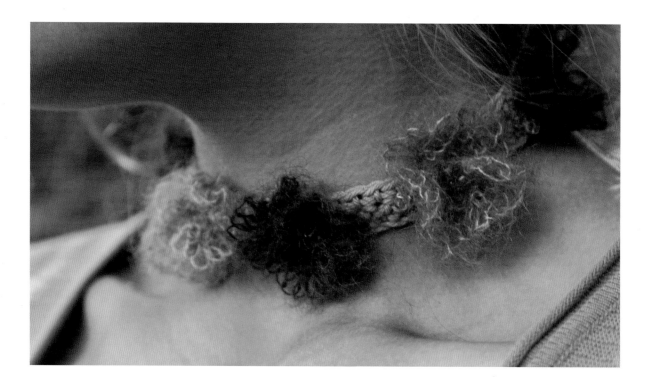

necklace

FLOWERS (make 7)

Using size 3 (3.25mm) needles and A, cast on 40 sts with lace cast-on method (see next page).

Row 1 (RS) K to end.

Row 2 K1, *skp; rep from * to last st, K1. *21 sts.*

Row 3 K1, *skp; rep from * to end. *11 sts.*

Do not bind off.

Cut off yarn, leaving a long yarn tail, thread this yarn tail onto a blunt-ended sewing needle and thread tail back through 11 sts on knitting needle, slipping sts off knitting needle as you proceed. Pull yarn end to gather sts and form a "rosette" shape, then secure yarn on WS of rosette.

Make 2 more flowers in A (for a total of 3 flowers in A), then make 4 in B in exactly same way.

CROCHET NECKLACE "CHAIN"

Using size D-3 (3mm) crochet hook and C, make a length of chain stitches almost long enough to fit loosely around your neck. (The ribbon ties will add to the final length of the necklace.)

Row 1 1 sc in 2nd ch from hook, 1 sc in each of rem ch, turn.

Row 2 Ch 1, 1 sc in each sc to end.

Fasten off.

TO FINISH NECKLACE

Weave in any yarn ends on the flowers and the crochet necklace "chain."

Sew the flowers in place along the choker, alternating the colors and securing each flower at the center with a cluster of three beads. Sew a cluster of three beads in place between each flower.

Cut two lengths of ribbon, each 12in/30cm long and sew one to each end of the necklace. Use these ribbons to tie on the necklace with a bow. If necessary, adjust the length of the ribbon.

bracelet

FLOWERS (make 5)

Make 5 flowers as for Necklace Flowers, working 2 in A and 3 in B.

CROCHET BRACELET "CHAIN"

Using size D-3 (3mm) crochet hook and C, make 27 chain stitches or a length of chain stitches almost long enough to fit loosely around your wrist. (The ribbon ties will add to the final length of the bracelet.)

Row 1 1 sc in 2nd ch from hook, 1 sc in each of rem ch, turn. *26 sc.*

Row 2 Ch 1, 1 sc in each sc to end.

Fasten off.

TO FINISH BRACELET

Weave in any yarn ends on the flowers and the crochet bracelet "chain."

Sew the flowers in place along the bracelet, alternating the colors and securing each flower at the center with a cluster of two or three beads.

Cut two lengths of ribbon, each 12in/30cm long and sew one to each end of the necklace. Use these ribbons to tie on the bracelet with a bow. If necessary, adjust the length of the ribbon.

corsage

FLOWERS (make 4)

Make 4 flowers as for Necklace Flowers, working 2 in A and 2 in B.

CORSAGE BASE

Using size D-3 (3mm) crochet hook and 2 strands of C held tog, make 6 chain stitches and join with a slip stitch to form a ring.

Round 1 (RS) Ch 1 (does NOT count as first sc), work

lace cast-on method

Also called the knit cast-on, this is a cast-on that gives a lacy, open edge. Since as a rule it is best to have a nice firm lower edge on knitting, the lace cast-on is not used often. The more popular thumb and cable cast-on methods give you a firm edge with a line along the lower edge (see pages 76 and 95). However, for lace, the work should look as if the lace just started—no line along the lower edge. Throughout the patterns in this book, I usually specify which kind of cast-on is best.

1 Make a slip knot as for any cast-on and place it on the left needle. Insert the right needle into the slip knot and knit the stitch in the usual way, but keep the slip knot on the left needle.

2 Insert the left needle into the resulting new stitch as shown by the arrow (from right to left through the front of the stitch) and slip it onto the left needle.

3 To make the next cast-on stitch, insert the right needle into the stitch just transferred back to the left needle, and knit a stitch in the usual way. Again, transfer this stitch back onto the left needle.

4 Repeat step 3 to make as many cast-on stitches as you need. If you want to tighten these cast-on loops, you can work into the back of each stitch on the first row—but for a lacy, open edge, work into the front of the cast-on stitches in the usual way.

1

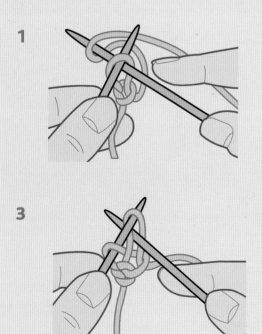

2

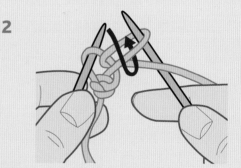

3

4

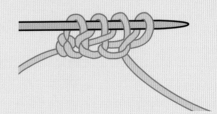

15 sc into ring, join with a slip stitch to first sc. *Do not turn at end of rounds, but work with RS always facing.*

Round 2 Ch 2 (counts as 1 sc and 1 ch), 1 sc in first sc in round below, ch 1, *1 sc in next sc, ch 1; rep from * to end of round, join with a slip stitch to first ch of round. *16 sc (counting first ch as first sc).*

Round 3 Ch 3 (counts as 1 sc and 2 ch), 1 sc in first sc in round below, ch 2, *1 sc in next sc, ch 2; rep from * to end of round, join with a slip stitch to first ch of round.

Round 4 Ch 4 (counts as 1 sc and 3 ch), 1 sc in first sc in round below, ch 3, *1 sc in next sc, ch 3; rep from * to end of round, join with a slip stitch to first ch of round. Fasten off.

Using size D-3 (3mm) crochet hook and 1 strand each of A and B held tog, join in new yarn and cont as follows:

Round 5 Join yarn with a slip stitch to any sc of last round, [ch 10, skip next sc, 1 slip stitch in next sc] 7 times, ch 10, skip next sc, join with a slip stitch to same sc as new yarn was joined into at beg of round. Fasten off.

TO FINISH CORSAGE

Weave in any yarn ends on the flowers and the crochet corsage base.

Sew the flowers in place on the round corsage base, alternating the colors and securing each flower at the center with a cluster of three beads.

Sew a large safety pin or brooch-back to the wrong side of the corsage.

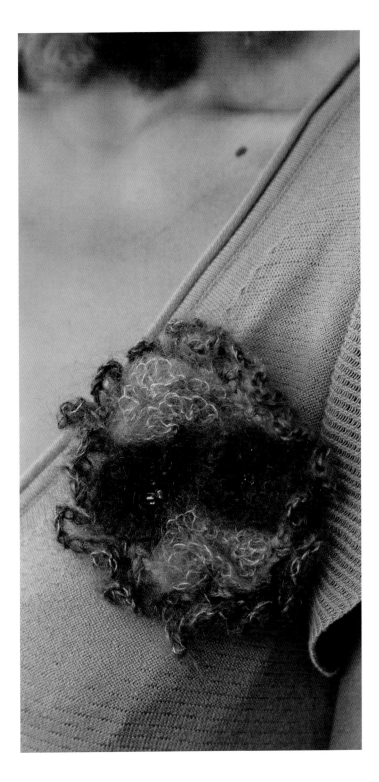

useful information

PRESSING AND AFTERCARE OF YOUR MOHAIR-MIX KNITTING

After knitting, some items will need to be pressed. Take care not to overdo this, as over-pressing can remove some of the lovely hazy mohair fluff. If you need to press, pin the knitting out to size and shape, with the wrong side up, on a thick towel on your board or work surface. Using a very slightly damp cloth and a cool iron, hover and skim the iron over the work, don't rest it on the cloth or press down. Remove the cloth and leave the work in place until it is dry.

Some items don't need pressing, such as the boas, and never press frills.

Because of their mohair content, and the delicate nature of mohair yarns, Rowan *Kidsilk Haze* and Rowan *Kidsilk Aura* must be hand washed. Most other mohair-mix yarns require the same treatment, so be sure to refer to the yarn label for yarn care instructions. Mohair simply longs to become felt and the merest whisper of hot water will cause it to do so. Do not rub or wring the items as this will also encourage felting or, at best, matting. Always follow the instructions on the yarn label. It is best to use cool water and a light wool wash liquid soap. There are some no-rinse solutions, or alternatively, rinse twice in cool water. I never use fabric softener on mohair.

After washing, gently squeeze out the excess water to get the weight off the knitting. If it's a big item, I lay it between two thick bath towels and gently press down on them to soak out more water.

Dry your knitting flat once you have reshaped it.

KNITTING ABBREVIATIONS

The following are the abbreviations used in this book. Special abbreviations are given with the patterns.

alt	alternate
approx	approximately
beg	begin(ning)
cm	centimeter(s)
cont	continu(e)(ing)
dec	decreas(e)(ing)
foll	follow(s)(ing)
g	gram(s)
garter st	garter stitch (knit every row)
in	inch(es)
inc	increase(e)(ing)
K	knit
LH	left hand
m	meter(s)
M1	make one stitch by picking up horizontal strand between stitch just knit and next stitch and working into back of this loop (one stitch increased)
mm	millimeter(s)
oz	ounce(s)
P	purl
patt	pattern; *or* work in pattern
psso	pass slipped stitch over
rem	remain(s)(ing)
rep	repeat(ing)
rev St st	reverse stocking stitch (purl all RS rows and knit all WS rows)
RH	right hand
RS	right side
skp	slip 1 knitwise, knit 1, pass slipped stitch over (one stitch decreased)
sl	slip
st(s)	stitch(es)

St st	stocking stitch (knit all RS rows and purl all WS rows)
tbl	through back of loop(s)
tog	together
WS	wrong side
yo	yarn over (yarn over RH needle to make a new stitch)

[ ] * Repeat instructions between square brackets, or after or between asterisks, as many times as instructed.

CROCHET ABBREVIATIONS

The simple crochet instructions in this book have been written using US crochet terminology. The UK equivalents for the US crochet terminology used in this book are as follows:

US	UK
chain (ch)	chain (ch)
single crochet (sc)	double crochet (dc)
skip (a stitch)	miss (a stitch)

YARN INFORMATION

The following are the specifications of the Rowan yarns used for the designs in this book (see page 118 for the yarn-weight symbols). It is always best to try to obtain the exact yarns specified in the patterns. If, however, you wish to find a substitute yarn, use the yarn descriptions given here to find a similar yarn type and yarn weight. When substituting yarn, remember to calculate the yarn amount needed by yardage/meterage rather than by ball weight.

For yarn care directions, refer to the yarn label.

Rowan Calmer

A lightweight cotton-mix yarn; 75 percent cotton, 25 percent acrylic/microfiber; 1³/₄oz/50g (approximately 175yd/160m) per ball; recommended gauge—21 sts and 30 rows to 4in/10cm measured over St st using size 8 (5mm) knitting needles.

Rowan 4-Ply Cotton

A super-fine-weight cotton yarn; 100 percent cotton; 1³/₄oz/50g (approximately 186yd/170m) per ball; recommended gauge—27–29 sts and 37–39 rows to 4in/10cm measured over St st using sizes 2–3 (3–3.25mm) knitting needles.

Rowan Kidsilk Aura

A medium-weight mohair-mix yarn; 75 percent kid mohair, 25 percent silk; ⁷/₈oz/25g (approximately 82yd/75m) per ball; recommended gauge—16–20 sts and 19–28 rows to 4in/10cm measured over St st using sizes 6–10 (4–6mm) knitting needles.

Rowan Kidsilk Haze

A lightweight mohair-mix yarn; 70 percent super kid mohair, 30 percent silk; ⁷/₈oz/25g (approximately 229yd/210m) per ball; recommended gauge—18–25 sts and 23–34 rows to 4in/10cm measured over St st using sizes 3–8 (3.25–5mm) knitting needles.

Rowan Scottish Tweed 4-Ply

A super-fine-weight wool yarn; 100 percent pure wool; ⁷/₈oz/25g (approximately 120yd/110m) per ball; recommended gauge—26–28 sts and 38–40 rows to 4in/10cm measured over St st using size 3 (3.25mm) knitting needles.

STANDARD YARN-WEIGHT SYSTEM

Categories of yarn, gauge ranges, and recommended knitting needle sizes from the Craft Yarn Council of America.
YarnStandards.com

Yarn-weight symbol and category names	0 LACE	1 SUPER FINE	2 FINE	3 LIGHT	4 MEDIUM	5 BULKY	6 SUPER BULKY
Types of yarns in category	fingering, 10-count crochet thread	sock, fingering, baby	sport, baby	DK, light worsted	worsted, afghan, Aran	chunky, craft, rug	bulky, roving
Knit gauge ranges* in St st to 4in (10cm)	33–40** sts	27–32 sts	23–26 sts	21–24 sts	16–20 sts	12–15 sts	6–11 sts
Recommended needle in metric size range	1.5–2.25 mm	2.25–3.25 mm	3.25–3.75 mm	3.7.5–4.5 mm	4.5–5.5 mm	6.5–8 mm	8mm and larger
Recommended needle in US size range	000 to 1	1 to 3	3 to 5	5 to 7	7 to 9	9 to 11	11 and larger

* **GUIDELINES ONLY** The above reflect the most commonly used gauges and needle sizes for specific yarn categories.
** Ultra-fine lace-weight yarns are difficult to put into gauge ranges; always follow the gauge given in your pattern for these yarns.

Rowan *Kidsilk Haze*

ROWAN YARN ADDRESSES

Contact the distributors listed here to find a supplier of Rowan hand knitting yarns (and fabrics) near you. For countries not listed, contact the main office in the UK or the Rowan website: **www.knitrowan.com**

USA
Westminster Fibers Inc.,
165 Ledge Street, Nashua,
NH 03060.
Tel: 1-800-445-9276.
E-mail: rowan@westminsterfibers.com
www.westminsterfibers.com

AUSTRALIA
Australian Country Spinners,
314 Albert Street, Brunswick,
Victoria 3056.
Tel: (61) 3 9380 3888.
Fax: (61) 3 9387 2674.
E-mail: sales@auspinners.com.au

AUSTRIA
Coats Harlander GmbH,
Autokaderstrasse 31, A-1210 Wien.
Tel: (01) 27716-0.
Fax: (01) 27716-228.

BELGIUM
Coats Benelux, Ring Oost 14A, Ninove,
9400. Tel: 0346 35 37 00.
E-mail: sales.coatsninove@coats.com

CANADA
Same as USA.

CHINA
Coats Shanghai Ltd., No. 9 Building,
Boasheng Road, Songjiang Industrial
Zone, Shanghai, 201613.
Tel: (86-21) 5774 3733.
Fax: (86-21) 5774 3768.

DENMARK
Coats Danmark A/S, Nannagade 28,
2200 Kobenhavn N.
Tel: 35 86 90 50.
Fax: 35 82 15 10.
E-mail: info@hpgruppen.dk
www.hpgruppen.dk

FINLAND
Coats Opti Oy, Ketjutie 3,
04220 Kerava.
Tel: (358) 9 274 871.
Fax: (358) 9 2748 7330.
E-mail: coatsopti.sales@coats.com

FRANCE
Coats France/Steiner Fréres,
SAS 100 avenue du Général de Gaulle,
18 500 Mehun-Sur-Yèvre.
Tel: 02 48 23 12 30.
Fax: 02 48 23 12 40.

GERMANY
Coats GMbH, Kaiserstrasse 1,
D-79341 Kenzingen.
Tel: 7644 8020.
Fax: 7644 802399.
www.coatsgmbh.de

HOLLAND
Same as Belgium.

HONG KONG
Coats China Holding Ltd.,
19/F Millenium City 2, 378 Kwun Tong
Road, Kwun Tong, Kowloon.
Tel: (852) 2798 6886.
Fax: (852) 2305 0311.

ICELAND
Storkurinn, Laugavegi 59,
101 Reykjavek.
Tel: (354) 551 8258.
E-mail: storkurinn@simnet.is

ITALY
Coats Cucirini srl, Via Sarca 223,
20126 Milano.
Tel: 800 992377.
Fax: 0266111701.
E-mail: servizio.clienti@coats.com

JAPAN
Puppy-Jardin Co. Ltd.,
3-8 11 Kudanminami, Chiyodaku,
Hiei Kudan Bldg. 5F, Tokyo.
Tel: (81) 3 3222-7076.
Fax: (81) 3 3222-7066.
E-mail: info@rowan-jaeger.com

KOREA
Coats Korea Co. Ltd., 5F Kuckdong B/D,
935-40 Bangbae-Dong,
Seocho-Gu, Seoul.
Tel: (82) 2 521 6262.
Fax: (82) 2 521 5181.
(*continued on next page*)

Rowan *Kidsilk Aura*

LEBANON
y.knot, Saifi Village,
Mkhalissiya Street 162,
Beirut.
Tel: (961) 1 992211.
Fax: (961) 1 315553.
E-mail: yknot@cyberia.net.lb

LUXEMBERG
Same as Belgium.

MEXICO
Estambres Crochet SA de CV,
Aaron Saenz 1891-7,
Monterrey, NL 64650.
Tel: +52 (81) 8335-3870.

NEW ZEALAND
ACS New Zealand,
1 March Place,
Belfast,
Christchurch.
Tel: 64-3-323-6665.
Fax: 64-3-323-6660.

NORWAY
Coats Knappehuset AS,
Pb 100 Ulset,
5873 Bergen.
Tel: (47) 55 53 93 00.
Fax: (47) 55 53 93 93.

SINGAPORE
Golden Dragon Store,
101 Upper Cross Street #02-51,
People's Park Centre, Singapore 058357.
Tel: (65) 6 5358454.
Fax: (65) 6 2216278.
E-mail: gdscraft@hotmail.com

SOUTH AFRICA
Arthur Bales PTY, P.O. BOX 44644,
62 4th Avenue, Linden 2104.
Tel: (27) 11 888 2401.
Fax: (27) 11 782 6137.

SPAIN
Oyambre, Pau Claris 145,
80009 Barcelona.
Tel: (34) 670 011957.
Fax: (34) 93 4872672.
E-mail: oyambre@oyambreonline.com

Coats Fabra, Sant Adria 20,
08030 Barcelona.
Tel: 93 2908400.
Fax: 93 2908409.
E-mail: atencion.clientes@coats.com

SWEDEN
Coats Expotex AB, Division Craft,
Box 297, 401 24 Göteborg.
Tel: (46) 33 720 79 00.
Fax: (46) 31 47 16 50.

SWITZERLAND
Coats Stroppel AG, Stroppelstrasse 16,
CH-5300 Tungi (AG).
Tel: 056 298 12 20.
Fax: 056 298 12 50.

TAIWAN
Cactus Quality Co. Ltd., P.O. Box 30
485, Taipei.
Office: 7Fl-2, No. 140, Roosevelt Road,
Sec 2, Taipei.
Tel: 886-2-23656527.
Fax: 886-2-23656503.
E-mail: cqcl@m17.hinet.net

THAILAND
Global Wide Trading,
10 Lad Prao Soi 88, Bangkok 10310.
Tel: 00 662 933 9019.
Fax: 00 662 933 9110.
E-mail: theneedleworld@yahoo.com

UK
Rowan, Green Lane Mill,
Holmfirth,
West Yorkshire HD9 2DX,
England.
Tel: +44 (0) 1484 681881.
Fax: +44 (0) 1484 687920.
E-mail: mail@knitrowan.com

author's acknowledgments

Grateful thanks to: Hilda, whose knitting skills, design eye and personal encouragement have been invaluable; Jean, for keeping me on track again and for your lovely work; to Rowan for giving me this fantastic opportunity; to Sharon for starting it all off and to all my lovely Rowan friends and colleagues, especially Sarah and Donna, my crochet-queens; to Susan, once again wise, patient and kind; John, whose photographs I adore, and Anne for her graphic skills and Sally for her careful editing; to Emma for the patience to check my patterns; to Jayne, Gemma, Lynne, and Nathalie for modeling; and to Marian, John, and Tessa for locations.